Acclaim for *The Postmodern Predicament*

"Bobby Angel offers a compelling commentary on our contemporary confusion and provides keen insights leading to a path forward. Anyone who wants an understandable introduction to philosophy (and hope for the future) will benefit greatly from reading this book."

—***Christopher West, Th.D.,*** President, Theology of the Body Institute

"Many professional philosophers write about abstractions that only matter to other philosophers, and many psychologists write about solutions that only make sense to other psychologists, but Bobby is guilty of neither. This book makes the history of disordered thought in our society understandable and points out a clear path forward that anyone can put into place."

—***Greg Bottaro, Psy.D.,*** Executive Director, CatholicPsych Institute and Author, *The Mindful Catholic: Finding God One Moment at a Time*

"This is a book to build a firm foundation in these tumultuous times. It is a work of great insight and hope. Angel has given us a gift in this exploration of how we have arrived at our current cultural moment and, more importantly, how we might find our way forward. Everybody is saying things are getting bad; Angel is giving us a roadmap to help us find our way.

My dear brothers and sisters, I highly recommend *The Postmodern Predicament* to anyone seeking to understand our times and to find a way to live with integrity and purpose. It is a book that will make you think, that will challenge you, and that will ultimately inspire you to seek the truth and to live it out in your daily life. Let us take up Bobby Angel's call to philosophize well, to seek wisdom, and to be beacons of hope in a world that often seems to have lost its way."

—***Fr. Agustino Torres, C.F.R.,*** Author, *Prepare Your Heart*

"Bobby Angel weaves through postmodernism's philosophical and cultural milieu and its dismal consequences. With his intelligent and quick-witted style, Angel awakens the reader to the underpinnings of a time of confusion, from the flattened-out boredom around us to the adventure of beauty."

—***Jared Zimmerer, Ph.D.,*** Director of Center for Catholic Media, Benedictine College

"Bobby Angel has taken the topic of philosophy, one we can often assume is only for certain types of readers, and, with sincerity and a profound simplicity, built a bridge that is integral for our times as we navigate a return to ourselves and God's plan for each of us. I'm grateful to Bobby for having the courage to write about what he loves; in doing so, he has given us a gift that will be valuable to readers today and for years to come."

—***Sr. Josephine Garrett,*** Sister of the Holy Family of Nazareth and Licensed Counselor

The Postmodern Predicament

Bobby Angel

THE POSTMODERN PREDICAMENT

and

a Roadmap for Recovery and Restoration

SOPHIA INSTITUTE PRESS
Manchester, New Hampshire

Cover design and image by: Enrique J. Aguilar

Sophia Institute Press
Box 5284, Manchester, NH 03108
1-800-888-9344
www.SophiaInstitute.com

Sophia Institute Press® is a registered trademark of Sophia Institute.

Hardcover ISBN 979-8-88911-250-1

ebook ISBN 979-8-88911-251-8

Library of Congress Control Number: 2024948546

First printing

To Jackie

"Men and women are on a journey of discovery which is humanly unstoppable—a search for the truth and a search for a person to whom they might entrust themselves."

—St. John Paul II, *Fides et Ratio*

Contents

PART 3
The Recovery

Foreword

DURING OUR HONEYMOON my wife and I had the privilege of spending several days in Paris, where we made it a point to visit the "big three" museums in the city.

The first was the one almost everyone knows about: the Louvre. It houses artworks from the ancient era up to the mid-nineteenth century, its most famous resident being *Mona Lisa*. The second was my personal favorite, the Orsay, which specializes in nineteenth-century French art and includes impressionists such as Monet and Van Gogh.

Then we visited Le Centre Pompidou, the museum dedicated to modern and especially postmodern art. However, one can only call it "art" if he stretches the meaning of that word to its breaking point.

Blank white canvases. A tire with a pole through it. A rock on top of a refrigerator.

It was garbage. Literally, one of the exhibits was just pieces of trash!

But from a "postmodern" perspective this is supposed to be a subversive exposé of what the world is really like, which is ironic coming from a mindset that rejects the idea that there can be absolute truth about anything.

Now, this would be amusing if postmodernism were confined to over-priced French museums. But we should be concerned that postmodernism infects centers of higher learning and think tanks that influence public policy. This can be seen in papers that defend ridiculous concepts like "feminist glaciology"—a feminist approach to studying glaciers.

In 1996 physics professor Alan Sokal decided to troll these postmodern elites by submitting a fake paper to the prestigious journal *Social Text*. Sokal's paper, entitled "Transgressing the Boundaries: Towards a Transformative Hermeneutics of Quantum Gravity," was full of purposefully absurd arguments and equivocations, such as confusing the "axiom of choice" in mathematical set theory with "pro-choice" support for legal abortion.

The journal's editors were briefly humiliated, but a movement that embraces humiliation as a virtue isn't so easily defeated. Granted, there is merit to exposing the vacuous nature of postmodern rhetoric as Sokal did. And there is some utility in simply pointing out these absurdities and exclaiming how "dumb" they are, but these kinds of strategies only take us so far.

As the history of ideas shows, when a paradigm shift occurs, what often happens is that a vacuum is left behind that can be filled with something even worse than what came before it. The rejection of the pure rationalism and empiricism of the so-called "Enlightenment" helped bring about the absurdities of postmodernism: Heaven help us if something worse takes the place of postmodernism if it is simply rejected without an appropriate substitute.

That's why I'm excited that Bobby Angel has written this book to show what's wrong with postmodernism and how we can escape its pervasive clutches. And not only that, but he also demonstrates how we can have a proper understanding of the classical understanding of objective truth, goodness, and beauty without sounding like theologians who are so untethered from regular life that they argue over how many angels can dance on the head of a pin.

In George Orwell's dystopian novel *1984*, a representative of the totalitarian government says, "There will be no distinction between beauty and ugliness. There will be no curiosity, no enjoyment of the process of life. All competing pleasures will be destroyed."

This is the great lie of postmodernism that is trumpeted in favor of a false egalitarianism. Bobby Angel shows us that true curiosity, the righteous pursuit of wisdom, is what we are all seeking, so that we can find the true joy in life for which each of us was beautifully and wonderfully made.

Trent Horn
Author, *Why We're Catholic*

PREFACE

THIS IS A book for people who find themselves supremely confused by the state of the culture in the West today and want a simple answer to "*How* did we get here?" And the important follow-up to that question, "What do we do about it?" For those answers, we'll have to turn to philosophy.

I had the good fortune of both teaching and serving as a campus minister at an all-boys high school for close to a decade. It was an incredible period of my life: freshly married, figuring out how to be a father to my first few children, and cutting my teeth on the daily grind of an educator. (I had significantly less gray hair than I do now.) It was a joy to accompany those young men with whom I was entrusted through seminars, retreats, and the tumultuous waters of maturing in their masculinity.

In my last few years in the classroom, I taught philosophy to the senior class. How does one make Socrates, Aquinas, Descartes, and friends matter to a seventeen- or eighteen-year-old? It was a challenge, and I relished it, for I had been blessed with professors who led me through the same quagmire. For my students I used video-game metaphors, movie references, and anything else I could to try and make sense of the complex topics that philosophers love speaking on: forms, logic, essences, ethics, being, meaning, nihilism, and so on. Some students enjoyed it, while other second-semester seniors understandably couldn't care less. "Will this be on the test?" is the exquisite question that makes every teacher's heart soar.

My hope was always that, at the end of the day, these young men would ultimately learn how to *think*, to ask questions, and to wonder again. Philosophy is literally the "love of wisdom," and Plato affirmed that it is "wonder" that is the starting point of all philosophy. To the person closed off to the world, arms crossed and mind shut in his or her own echo chamber, wonder has died and jaded cynicism reigns. "Unless you change and become like children, you will never enter the kingdom of heaven," Christ asserted to His followers (Matt. 18:3, NRSVCE), and this gestures not only toward the spiritual gift of faith (trust) but also to a mind open to adventure.

Children, naturally curious, are not afraid to ask questions and wonder at the world, always ready to ask that incessantly wonderful question, *Why?* It's a shame that we in the Western world have become so cocooned by comfort that we have ceased to wonder. The urge to explore, experiment, and explode with creativity is so often missing from our youth today. I'll reference the effects of our technological revolution in a later chapter, but suffice to say that philosophy only makes sense, and will only find importance in your life, if you are able to ask questions with curiosity once again.

The bottom line that I would always come back to with my students was this: *the ideas we hold have consequences*. If we think life has value and truth can be known, we will live as such and our behaviors (and our laws) will reflect that. If we have been told that God doesn't exist, then we start to live like practical atheists and morality is simply what I make of it. If we are authors of our own reality, then mere biology is a limitation and we will attempt to overrule Mother Nature at every turn. If we believe that we are known and loved by God and have been called to spread the good news of Jesus' redemptive act of dying in our place for our sins so that we might have new life, we eagerly send missionaries to every continent possible in order to proclaim Christ.

One day in class I reviewed the four big movements of philosophical history: ancient, medieval, modern, and postmodern. I will sketch these out more thoroughly in the book's first portion. I noted to my students how, very broadly speaking, the ancients were concerned with what was the *nature* of truth, the medievals believed that *God* was the unifying Truth, the moderns became obsessed with proving with *certainty* what was empirically true, and we've now arrived in a postmodern time that largely asserts there is *no truth*.

After some silence, with more than a few glazed eyes staring back at me, one student insightfully spoke up.

"Mr. Angel, it's like we're back at the *beginning* of philosophy again. We don't even know what is true anymore."

I leaned against the whiteboard, stunned by this seventeen-year-old's insight. This young man understood the landscape before him. We are now in this strange wasteland of great material and technological wealth but spiritual impoverishment and philosophical turmoil. We have amassed great comfort but have lost the point of living. To the extent that we continue to deny objective reality and live incoherently with everyone's "own truth," we are further running our civilizational ship aground. Unmoored from a deeper sense of meaning and direction, it's no coincidence that this current generation is suffering from such widespread anxiety and depression.

We are back at the beginning, indeed.

But we are never beyond hope. While many feel rudderless and the temptation to despair is real, the truth can be known and has revealed itself within the person of Christ, who is the same yesterday, today, and forever, and continues to be at work in the world throughout the ages.

We certainly can't put the postmodern genie back in the bottle. Much as people might want to try to return to the worldviews of the past—of the Founding Fathers' rationalism or Thomas Aquinas's scholasticism—sadly, it can't be done. Others delight in the brave new world that is being constructed by demolishing the old in real time before our eyes—yet many I've met can't articulate what the goal is we're "progressing" toward.

What is for certain is that we have been called to live in the age where God has placed us, with all its challenges and blessings.

If we are going to proclaim truth to the world, we first have to get to the truth.

Even if the truth seems lost, even if truth has been trampled underfoot, even if it seems truth has been shelled and left for dead in a pile of rubble, truth is still there. And the truth will have the final say. It's not that there is a new or different truth to be unearthed, but rather that we have been tasked with rediscovering the truth (or learning it for the first time) and allowing it to convict us. When truth takes over, we will be its defenders and proclaimers, even unto death.

This is why Pope St. John Paul II said, "All men and women ... are in some sense philosophers and have their own philosophical conceptions with which they direct their lives."[1] We have a *duty* as Christians—as human beings—to philosophize. Really, we're

1 John Paul II, Encyclical Letter on Faith and Reason *Fides et Ratio* (September 14, 1998), no. 30, https://www.vatican.va/content/john-paul-ii/en/encyclicals/documents/hf_jp-ii_enc_14091998_fides-et-ratio.html.

going to philosophize whether we like it or not. So, why not philosophize well?

We might be philosophically starting "back at the beginning" in many ways, but we're not starting from scratch. It is the prophetic voices up and down history, who call us to be set apart and remember what is true, who can inspire us to live well today. They call us to love what is true and fight for the people who are caught up in disordered ideas and the wages of sin (which includes *all* of us).

This book is the fruit of my own philosophical journey and education, my time spent teaching in the classroom and accompanying young people in varied ministerial settings, and my continued desire to understand the ideas that drive the politics and culture of our day. I'll be drawing from the lives and teachings of various philosophers, giving the "short and sweet" takeaways from some of these very complicated thinkers. I also have an appendix in the back to point to some great books for those who want to go deeper.

Beyond naming the problem and understanding the lay of our land, I'm also concerned with how we navigate a path forward. Not everything that postmodernity has brought us is necessarily to be discarded. Throughout these chapters, I'll sketch out the ideas that undergird our contemporary situation, note the positives that have emerged alongside the confusion, and in the third section of the book suggest some ideas and solutions for moving forward.

Believe it or not, wheat still grows among the tares. Take heart and know that the God who has allowed us to arrive here is still guiding all things and will bring our work to His desired completion.

Above all, remember to wonder, and be not afraid to ask that delightful question, *Why?*

Bobby Angel
Feast of the Triumph of the Cross
Anno Domini 2023

Acknowledgments

Thank you to the fine people at Sophia Institute Press for their guidance and patience on this project.

Thank you to my beautiful wife, Jackie, for her steadfast support, to my parents and family for walking with me on this journey of wonder, and to my children for their patience while I worked away at the computer.

Thank you to the Cistercians of Our Lady of Dallas Abbey for allowing me to retreat on their grounds for prayer and the writing of this book.

Thank you to my past students and for the administration of Servite High School for entrusting me to teach philosophy and to lead young men to our Lord.

Thank you to the professors and priest-professors of my seminary studies who helped me wrapped my head around philosophy in the first place.

THE POSTMODERN PREDICAMENT

Part 1

The Story

Chapter 1

Why?

Philosophy begins in wonder, according to the ancient minds, and it all starts with that question, *Why?*

I mean this in reference to both the history of philosophy and to my three-year-old's stance toward anything I ask her to do.

"Esther, we have to get in the car."

"Why?" she asks, doing her emerging childhood duty.

"Because we need to get going."

"Why?"

"Because we're going to be late."

"Why?"

"Because it's rude to be late."

"Why?"

"Because time is valuable, and other people's time is valuable."

"Why?"

"Because we want to honor other people and time is finite."

"Why?"

"Because we are made in the image and likeness of God, and one day our time will be done and we'll die."

"Why?"

"Because . . . it's a mystery."

"Ok. Let's go, Daddy."

This more-or-less exact transcript of a hurried conversation with my toddler is a snapshot of the curious mind that has yet to shut down due to cynicism or the sad state of malaise that trouble the average adult's mind. The beautifully incessant question "Why?" is a hallmark of the human mind. It's not enough to see or know *that* a thing works—we want to know *how* it works and *why* it works in the first place.

Why is it here and *what* is its purpose?

Why am I here and what is my purpose?

If you're still willing to entertain and ask those questions, and pursue them to their end, you're doing philosophy! And what's more, you are in good company.

You may have heard the expression "ideas have consequences," and this is a key component of any human thought. To the extent that we allow a central idea about the purpose of human life, what a good life looks like, or whether it's reasonable to believe in God, that idea can guide all our actions and decisions.

The 2010 movie *Inception* demonstrates this concept in action quite well. The film imagines the science-fiction premise that not only could someone enter the dreams of another person, but that he or she could also plant an idea in that person's dreams. "An idea is like a virus, resilient, highly contagious," the protagonist (played by Leonardo DiCaprio) notes. "The smallest seed of an idea can grow. It can grow to define or destroy you."

Chapter 2

The Philosopher Pope

In my twenties I spent three years of my life in seminary formation, surrendering my life to Christ to see if I was called to the vocation of the Catholic priesthood. I eventually felt the call to marriage and met my now-wife, with whom I've shared more than ten years of marriage and five children here on this earth (as of this writing). But in my seminary studies, I was blessed with extended time to learn philosophy from some amazing professors and instructors. These men filled in the gaps contained within a purely secular approach to the history of philosophy.

You might wonder why a potential priest would need to know philosophy (and that would be a great question to ask, like my three-year-old's "Why?"). You wouldn't be the first to wonder. "What does Athens have in common with Jerusalem?" the third-century Christian thinker Tertullian wrote, "The academy with the Church?"[2] The discipline of philosophy can seem like an esoteric exercise or even, for a believing Christian, a "step backward," when compared with the power of God's revelation of Himself.

From the Catholic Christian perspective, philosophy still holds great value. Before we ever got to God and the formal study

[2] Tertullian, *De Praescriptione Haereticorum*, VIII, 9: SC 46, 98: "*Quid ergo Athenis et Hierosolymis? Quid academiae et ecclesiae?*"

of theology, we had to start with what it means to be *human*, and this involved the questions of philosophy. Medieval thinkers consider philosophy to be the "handmaiden" to theology, indicating a subservient position, yes, but also that it is important as an assistant to theology. Many Christians today, without a grounding understanding of the human person, are being swept to and fro by a culture that changes its mind every fifteen minutes on time-tested values.

It was actually a careful reading of St. John Paul II's encyclical letter *Fides et Ratio: On the Relationship Between Faith and Reason* in my first year of seminary that helped to bring together so much of the scattered thinking I'd adopted, growing up in our fragmented culture. Right out of the gate, the future saint wrote, "Faith and reason are like two wings on which the human spirit rises to the contemplation of truth; and God has placed in the human heart a desire to know the truth—in a word, to know himself, so that, by knowing and loving God, men and women may also come to the fullness of truth about themselves."[3]

Aside from the poetic lyricism of our former pontiff, did you catch that the word *truth* was used three times? John Paul II asserted that we were designed as men and women to (1) contemplate the truth, (2) seek and know God, who is the Truth, and (3) understand more deeply the truth about ourselves. This isn't pie-in-the-sky optimism or a mere romantic ideal. John Paul II drank deeply of both philosophy and theology. He suffered under both the Nazi and Communist regimes that overtook his native Poland; he had a front-row seat to how bad or degrading philosophies carry drastic consequences for the human person. He was also a man of profound prayer who led the charge to

[3] John Paul II, *Fides et Ratio*, preface.

boldly reclaim the culture for Christ, noting that the sciences have nothing to fear from faith and vice versa.

Truth can be known and ought to be pursued. I will continue to draw on the insights of St. John Paul II from this rich encyclical as we move forward through a survey of the history of philosophy.

The word philosophy comes from the Greek *philos,* meaning "friend," and *sophia*, meaning "wisdom." Many philosophers, including John Paul II, were earnest seekers of what is true in this world and how to live in accordance with it. Some philosophers, though, were not so much seekers as they were interested in wordplay and dallying with ideas detached from questions of reality. And other thinkers were more focused on deconstructing the very scaffolding they were standing upon—some gleefully, others with great seriousness. We'll meet such characters throughout the course of this book.

And—surprise! Even if you "hate" philosophy and think that asking such questions is ultimately a meaningless endeavor, you're still *doing* philosophy. If you think life is purposeless, that there is no God, *that's* your philosophy. That core idea will dictate how you see and operate in the world. Companies and organizations have *philosophies* (misused as that term might be, at times), which explain their core values and set their directional compass in the world. Anarchists and apathetics alike live by a philosophy of what they consider to be valuable (or not), what pursuits to follow, or what questions to ask or not ask. You can't escape philosophy!

So, *how did we get here?* How did we start to think the thoughts we think, and when? How did we arrive at the state we're in as twenty-first-century citizens of the Western world, a state that's in such destabilizing flux and can seem so disorienting and aimless? How did we come to a stage where people declare with utter seriousness that "their truth" trumps "your truth"?

I want to take you now on a survey across the four broad philosophical eras of history to highlight their major thinkers and beliefs, so that we can put our story into a larger context. As stated in this book's preface, this is a brief flyover of these brilliant minds and their work; there's an appendix in the back for anyone who wants to go deeper into either recommended resources or the primary texts themselves.

Chapter 3

The Ancients

THE HISTORY OF Western philosophy begins in ancient Greece, from the fifth to the third centuries B.C. Many of us know the names of Socrates, Plato, and Aristotle, even if we don't know a lick of what they actually taught or wrote. These figures have been immortalized in marble busts and classical paintings, and there is a good chance that when we think about the classical study of philosophy, we imagine bearded, toga-clad figures such as these three men.

Socrates never wrote anything down. All we know about his teachings and thoughts comes from the dutiful writings of his students, most notably Plato. Socrates asked questions—*lots* of questions. "Socratic seminars" today are based on his formula of inquiry. No subject was off-limits. Any idea could be probed, and no one, not even a statesman, was exempt from critical thinking.

Socrates especially enjoyed taking on the Sophists, teachers and rhetoricians who set themselves up as masters of persuasion and argument and who were generally more concerned with winning debates and less about whether or not their arguments were *true*. All we have is *opinions* about the matters of what is outside of us, they claimed. For instance, this water might be cold to you but warm to me; each person is the only judge of it, according to the Sophist. The Sophists were some of the very first skeptics and relativists. Mostly they were professional tutors, serving wealthy Greek households and growing quite rich indeed. Socrates, meanwhile, refused payment and remained poor. He also grew infamous by his incessant prodding of the Sophists' intellectual laziness, shaming the Greek elite by extension.

In Plato's *Apology*, he notes Socrates's conviction that "the unexamined life is not worth living" and that the care for one's soul is of utmost importance. To know thyself, to know what is good and true and try to move toward that goal is vital. Socrates believed that the doctrine of relativism would make us lazy, faint-hearted, and worse off in the long run.

His continual questioning eventually landed him in hot water with the local government of Athens and he was accused of "corrupting the city's youth." In 399 B.C., Socrates was made to drink a poison called hemlock as punishment and died. He kept his cool, his courage, and even his ironic sense of humor to the end. When a disciple named Apollodorus exclaimed his difficulty in seeing Socrates put to death unjustly, Socrates quipped, "My beloved Apollodorus, was it your preference to see me put to death justly?"[4]

Plato

Socrates's student Plato would take up the mantle of inquiry to do his teacher proud. It is the thinking of Plato, and his future student Aristotle, that grounds the entire tradition of Western philosophy. From Plato, we receive a plethora of writings (usually with Socrates as the main character), and aside from his brilliant

[4] Xenophon, *Apology 28*, trans. O. J. Todd, in *Xenophon IV*, ed. E. C. Marchant and O. J. Todd (Cambridge, MA: Harvard University Press, 1979).

political work, *The Republic*, one of his most well-known stories is his "Allegory of the Cave."

In a nutshell, Plato tells the story of a man who has been shackled all his life in a cave and thinks that the shadows on the walls are "reality." Somehow he escapes and, after adjusting to the terror of the outside world's blinding light, understands the nature of true reality and desires to return to the cave to break the chains of his fellow prisoners still shackled to their falsehoods. (*The Matrix* film is a modern retelling of this allegory. It's also where we get the colloquial term "red pilled," meaning that one has awoken to reality and no longer lives in a comfortable delusion.)

Of course, not all the prisoners in the cave believe or even welcome their estranged tribesman back into their home. This is where Plato's allegory is also a tribute to his teacher Socrates and his doomed attempt to bring the light of truth to those chained in darkness. Some people warm up to the truth, while for others the truth is threatening; thus, those who risk sharing the truth are met with indifference, castigation, or even violence.

An important concept also begins to form for these early thinkers: *logos*. It's a rich word, having a host of potential meanings. It can mean the principle of balance, a force of life and intelligence that somehow penetrates the cosmos, or even the higher, unseen spiritual world.

For Plato, the "really real" of this world was not the earthly shell of existence but seeking after this *logos* and entering this world of "the Forms." According to Plato, the Forms are the prototypes of everything we see. Each chair is an imperfect realization of an ideal chair, the "Form" of chair. The point of seeking truth, in the end, is to contemplate virtue (excellence in habit and living) and for the soul to escape the fleeting material world and reach the world of the Forms. Plato would agree with Yoda from *The Empire*

Strikes Back: "Luminous beings are we, not this crude matter." This Platonic ideal of the soul being the "real us" that needs to escape the body manifests itself up and down the centuries and is alive and well today.

In Raphael's famous painting *The School of Athens*, two figures hold center stage, walking through the archways and passing through a marketplace of mathematicians and other brilliant minds. Plato, on the left, points up toward the heavens at what he considers to be of value, and on the right is Aristotle, a student of Plato, whose palm faces downward to emphasize the concrete things of the material world. Aristotle emphasized the "crude matter" that Plato was quick to move beyond, seeing the particulars of reality as more important to discerning the truth than abstract "forms."

We have Aristotle to thank for his studies of physical sciences, for empirical categorizations such as "primary substances," and for considering what made up something's *essence* versus its *existence* (a dragon or unicorn, for instance, has a common *essence*, which is how we can categorize it; whether or not a dragon or unicorn *exists* is a different matter). Plato, on the other hand, thought the senses were not to be trusted in one's search for true knowledge. Aristotle emphasized the study of the natural world and believed that human understanding begins with sense perception.

But Aristotle was also not a cold scientist. He believed in the soul and that the intellect (*nous*) has the capacity to grasp universal truths. Like Plato, Aristotle also believed that for all things there was a *telos*, a purpose and final goal for which they have been designed. Aristotle also articulated the concept of the Unmoved Mover, a supreme being in pure form who stood outside of time and space in order for time and space to exist in the first place. For Aristotle, this was more of an intellectual necessity than a religious conviction. He could conceive of no other way to explain the existence of the universe—of existence itself.

Now of course there were pre-Socratic (i.e., before Socrates) thinkers and plenty of other budding philosophers asking key questions about life, the afterlife, and the nature of reality. The renowned mathematician Pythagoras lived over a hundred years before Socrates, around the same time as the Buddha was conceptualizing his path to enlightenment in the East. There were also notable Roman philosophers such as Seneca and movements such as cynicism and stoicism, the latter of which is enjoying a resurgence today. But Socrates, Plato, and Aristotle remain "the Big Three" of the ancient world, and it is upon their foundation that the discipline of philosophy began constructing its house.

The thinkers of the ancient world were beginning to articulate that the universe was knowable, logical, and operated by certain observable principles. Rather than rejecting the myths and stories of their time, these first philosophers curiously opened up their minds to new explanations of why reality is the way it is.

Chapter 4

The Medievals

The medieval time period is an important era in the history of philosophy, but one that is rarely taught. When I took a general philosophy course in my undergraduate studies, this period was simply skipped over entirely as if nothing of importance happened for 1500 years. Often brushed aside as the backward "Dark Ages," a time of barbarianism and superstition, the medieval era is a crucial period in the history of philosophy that deserves attention and study.

Part of the struggle for our contemporary minds to properly understand or appreciate these Middle Ages is that the greatest minds of this time had their philosophy deeply *intertwined* with their religious faith. Instead of two separated disciplines of study, there existed a "great synthesis" of faith and philosophy. C. S. Lewis, who served as chair of Medieval and Renaissance Literature at Magdalene College, Cambridge, referred to the medieval synthesis as "the Model," because it entailed a deep harmony between Heaven and Earth.

Whether one is a believer or not, it must be acknowledged that the person of Jesus Christ and the resulting movement of Christianity almost two thousand years ago forever changed the world—and this includes the history of philosophy. Jesus' disciples-turned-apostles went out to lands far and wide to build up a new people of believers. As the early believers went out, they encountered the cultures and philosophies of both East and West, appealing to common ground and performing signs and wonders.

After the conversion of Emperor Constantine in 312, Christianity went from a persecuted fringe of ragtag believers to a state-sanctioned religion of notoriety. Bishops became privileged leaders and began the construction of beautiful basilicas. Of course, there would later be problems of the Church and the state becoming too tightly intertwined. Wherever there are sinful humans there will be hypocritical or corrupt leadership. But for now it's worth noting the ascendancy of Christianity and the emerging Christendom that would stabilize, in particular, the European continent, and which would by its nature influence the study of philosophy through the Renaissance of the fifteenth and sixteenth centuries.

Now some leaders of the early Church wanted nothing to do with philosophy, asserting that this was a step "backward" for faith in Christ. But several Church Fathers, such as Origen, adopted Platonic philosophy, and perhaps most noteworthy was St. Augustine (354–430), who first immersed himself in the philosophies of his time as he was living a life of debauchery in his youth. After a radical conversion to belief in Christ, Augustine succeeded in producing arguably the first great synthesis of philosophy and theology, grounding the knowledge of Plato in the Scriptures and the revelation of Christ.[5] For hundreds of years, Augustine was *the* intellectual heavyweight in the philosophical tradition.

Anselm of Canterbury (1033–1109) picked up the torch through his writings and saintly example. Anselm asserted that faith is not in competition with the search for reason, for God

[5] John Paul II, *Fides et Ratio*, no. 40.

designed us as rational creatures and thus we have nothing to fear from using our intellects well. The desire for truth spurs reason to go further, and mature faith need not be afraid of questioning. *Credo ut intelligam*, "Faith seeks understanding," as Anselm beautifully wrote. From the beginning of his *Proslogium*: "I long to understand in some degree thy truth, which my heart believes and loves. For I do not seek to understand that I may believe, but I believe in order to understand."

We in the contemporary world have switched the equation: I must understand if I should ever dare to believe. Of course, it is important to ask questions and discern what is true of any idea, political statement, or religious dogma. But Anslem notes that we must start by having the wonder of Socrates and the curiosity of a child in order to understand later. We all start with the foundation of *trust* (which is a type of faith, by the way), in either our caregivers to meet our basic needs, our teachers to be our reliant guides, or that my car will appropriately start when I put the keys in the ignition. Faith is exercised on a daily basis all around us, and in no way contradicts the use of reason.

In the medieval era, philosophy also encompassed what we call today the *sciences*—psychics, biology, astronomy, geology, and so forth. The love of wisdom involved the whole of creation! Philosophy had yet to become the abstract, disembodied, and caricatured version that we know today.

The philosophers of the medieval era were gritty. While they took supernatural matters quite seriously, its major thinkers also had their hands in the dirt and muck of the time in order to harvest much fruit. Barbarians and Vikings were actively confronted and fought off. The pagans who converted to Christianity were instructed in forgiveness, humility, and compassion as well as monotheism. There were also substantial writings in this period from the Islamic philosophers Avicenna (Ibn Sinā) and Averroës (Ibn Rushd) and from Jewish philosophers like Moses Maimonides, which substantially influenced Christian philosophy.

The medieval influence of the Church can be noticeably observed in its care for the human person. The Christian understanding that man and woman have been created "in the image and likeness of God" (the *imago Dei*) began to permeate society. Hospitals were created to care for the sick and discarded, and great universities were founded all over Europe. Feast days were established, Gregorian chant developed, and massive Gothic cathedrals were constructed. These advances were, truly, a product of Christian philosophy.

Whether or not one believes that Christianity as a religion is true, the very security and flowering of Western civilization owed its existence to the strength of the Christian Church.[6] If you believe that human life should be valued and that the weakest of society ought to be protected, you have the Catholic Church and the concept of the *imago Dei* to thank.

St. Thomas Aquinas

We can't leave a discussion of the medieval period without giving a little extra attention to one of this era's heavy hitters, St. Thomas Aquinas.

An Italian friar and theologian of the thirteenth century, Thomas is the most well-known medieval scholar. As a young man, he felt called to join the Dominicans, a new medicant order established by St. Dominic Guzman that emphasized poverty, preaching, teaching, and begging for alms. His family attempted

[6] Richard Tarnas, *The Passion of the Western Mind: Understanding the Ideas That Have Shaped Our World View* (New York: Ballantine Books, 1991), 169.

to stop his vocation, but Thomas persisted and his family eventually relented.

In his education at the University of Paris, Thomas encountered the newly rediscovered works of Aristotle and, despite the concern among various Church authorities about incorporating philosophies of reason into the faith, studied and eventually lectured on the Greek sages. With his sharp intellect, Thomas rose in notoriety and wrote extensively to demonstrate the reasonableness of faith. He drew up Aristotle's observations of the natural world to show the harmony of not just faith and reason, but also the soul and the body, working against the long-held notion that the body and the natural world were degraded and without value (a notion which, ironically, stemmed largely from a certain reading of Plato).

His two most sizable works, the *Summa Theologiae* and the *Summa Contra Gentiles*, still stand as well-respected resources in classical theology. He also worked tirelessly, teaching against errors, devoting himself to prayer, and trying to repair the schism between the Latin and Greek churches. Thomas's work helped to stabilize Christendom "when the discovery of Greek science, culture, and thought seemed about to crush it."[7] He died in 1274 and was declared a saint in 1323.

Many have made the connection that if Augustine baptized the works of Plato, then Thomas Aquinas baptized the works and thought of Aristotle. It's a broad generalization, but it's also mostly true. Thomas did not consider himself a philosopher, but he had great respect for the thinkers of the past—especially Aristotle, whom he often quotes simply as "the philosopher." Thomas honors

[7] Marie-Dominique Chenu, "Legacy of St. Thomas Aquinas," Britannica, last updated August 1, 2024, https://www.britannica.com/biography/Saint-Thomas-Aquinas/Legacy.

the role of reason and its great capacity to make sense of existence, while noting that the divine revelation of God through Jesus Christ meets and perfects man's finite mind. In his *Summa Theologica* he famously outlined five "ways" (or "proofs") we can philosophically deduce God's existence from the world around us, along with offering a great many other profound insights.

Thomas drew upon Aristotle's focus on essences and the substances of things (what is the essence of a chair, or "chairness"?), while also adding the importance of existence into the conversation. Thomas aligns with Aristotle in the belief that we start with our sensory experience of the world to make sense of it, because we are material beings experiencing the world around us. By contrast, Plato, Augustine, and Anselm lean toward our souls having some "memory" of the divine world above, with the goal of escaping the imperfections of the body. There is something integral about the unity of the body/soul composite for the human person, according to Thomas, for we are not destined to be disembodied spirits. This fact points us toward Christ's Resurrection from the dead, a fact established not by abstract reason but by revelation.

Finally, Aquinas defines true happiness as consisting in total immersion in absolute goodness forever: the Beatific Vision of seeing God "face-to-face." Philosophy can offer hints and echoes of this destination but, for Aquinas, only God's grace can supply such an unmerited gift.

Not everyone bought into Aquinas's grand harmony between the tenets of religion and the capacities of reason, though. This takes us to the next great epoch of Western history, the transition from the medieval into the modern era.

Chapter 5

The Moderns

There is no clean "break" as to when the medieval period ends and the modern period begins, but by the 1500s, the foundation of the "Great Synthesis" of philosophy and theology was showing signs of stress. The Model was beginning to crack.

Ever since St. Augustine fought off the skeptics of the late 300s, there had been general agreement that the human person could grasp and comprehend the truth. God, through His aid in divine revelation, met our natural faculties and helped to "complete the circuit" so the human person could now live in a coherent framework of "the good life." This paved the way for Aquinas and his contemporaries to harmonize faith and reason, the spiritual and the physical world, in a comprehensive way that stabilized the European continent.

But some figures sought (whether intentionally or unintentionally) to revive skepticism toward our capacity to know reality. Born shortly after Aquinas's death, British priest and philosopher William of Ockham, for instance, is a figure who bridges the medieval and modern periods. Ockham took an alternate approach to Aquinas's confidence in the harmony of reason and divine revelation, instead emphasizing the human person's limits in grasping universal truths. God was so far *beyond* us, he argued, that we should turn our eyes to the material world alone and not make arrogant speculations about invisible realities or universal essences.

Ockham went so far as to deny the reality of abstract ideas outside the human mind and our structure of language, thus giving new force to a form of thinking call *nominalism*. Nominalism (from the Latin *nominalis*, meaning "names") holds that the essences or beings of things ("dogness" or "chairness") do not actually exist anywhere but are simply external projections that we make sense of through our language. A "tree" might as well be called something like "zargplat," since it's just a word to describe something that's there in front of me. Likewise, any connection we draw between one tree and another exists solely in our own minds. There's no such thing as a tree *per se*; this is simply a name or word category we invent in an attempt to simplify the world around us and make it more comprehensible to our limited intellects. This concept of nominalism blossomed in radical ways during our contemporary era in which concepts like "woman" or even "truth" are declared to be mere "constructs" and denied wholesale.

Ockham's ideas spread throughout the universities in the fourteenth century, and so the early embers of the modern era—especially the new separation of the secular and religious disciplines—began to be inflamed and the underlying medieval worldview that harmonized Christian doctrine and Aristotle's wisdom would soon be discarded on the ash heap. The tragic fruit of Ockham's work was a lasting rift between religion (theology) and the sciences (philosophy). By trying to preserve the purity of Christian doctrine and keep it "untainted" by other studies, Ockham snapped the connective thread Aquinas worked so hard to construct.

The great synthesis of medieval philosophy and theology began to splinter apart.

✠ ✠ ✠

For the families, rulers, clergy, and thinkers of the fourteenth through the nineteenth centuries, it was an epoch of discoveries, unimagined technological advances, and unsettling new questions. Entire continents suddenly came into existence and advances in the sciences unsettled long-held beliefs about how the cosmos operated.

Within one generation there were the masterworks of Leonardo, Michelangelo, and Raphael, a rebellion against the Catholic Church by Martin Luther which began the Reformation, and the kickstarting of the Scientific Revolution by Copernicus.[8] It was a cocktail of excitement and disorientation. Whereas the medieval thinkers segmented time into *Before Christ* (B.C.) and *Anno Domini* (A.D.), the modern thinkers declared that they were in the triumphant "third act" of a tripartite structure of history: ancient, medieval, and finally modernity, the high point of human history—at least according to us moderns!

The Renaissance was an exciting blend of all sorts of human disciplines: math, mechanics, astronomy, beauty and art, to name a few, and this era produced some of the most beautiful paintings known to the world. The eighteenth century, in particular, is often described as "the Enlightenment," as its thinkers began to glory in the pursuit of pure reason detached from any kind of religious or supernatural sensibilities.

Note the wording, by the way, of "enlightenment," as if those living in that period were suddenly emancipated from the oppressive structures of the Church and her "dark ages." The American Catholic philosopher Peter Kreeft notes that the term "is ironic; for spiritually the eighteenth century was the darkest ever. Scientism and rationalism replaced faith; the human heart narrowed

8 Tarnas, *Passion of the Western Mind*, 224.

and hardened in conformity with its own gods, the inventions of its own hands."[9] These are the brush strokes of the story that have stuck with us.

Now we come to Martin Luther, the Augustinian monk whom we now regard as the father of the Protestant Reformation. Like his hero, Augustine, Luther is principally remembered as a theologian, but he made a decisive contribution to the trajectory of Western philosophy as well.

Luther was deeply influenced by Ockham's intellectualism, which led him to question the highly rational dogmas of the Catholic Church. Luther and his fellow Reformers, Huldrych Zwingli and John Calvin, also took Ockham's premise further by asserting that God is wholly *separate* and set-apart from humanity, and that the human person is not fundamentally good, as Aquinas and the Catholic Church taught and the new secular humanists believed, but utterly depraved and perverse. In their view, we shouldn't trust our own minds, our freedom, the Vatican, or any other authority.

Therefore, the Reformation movement, along with the larger fracturing of European Christendom, had two secondary effects. First, it further untethered theology from philosophical inquiry, a connection that Augustine and Aquinas had worked to establish. Secondly, it advanced the primacy of the individual over subordination to a larger Church authority, thus paving the way for the radical individualism that would mark Western thought moving forward. It's worth noting that a man who placed so much emphasis on the individual believer had such a low opinion of humanity—including himself.

9 Peter Kreeft, *Back to Virtue: Traditional Moral Wisdom for Modern Moral Confusion* (San Francisco: Ignatius Press, 1992), 55.

✠ ✠ ✠

"I think, therefore I am."

You may know this pithy expression, which comes from the pen of René Descartes (1596–1650), a man who is often held up as the "father of modern philosophy." It could be argued that this new epoch of thought crystallized with his emphasis on clarity, a move that helped solidify the trajectory of philosophy and science fully apart from theology and faith.

In the early seventeenth century, Descartes set out on his own journey to blaze a new philosophical trail. A gifted but bored student, Descartes, schooled by the Jesuits of his native France, surmised that a new method was needed in order to reach certainty—in a most uncertain time—about what could be considered reliable and trustworthy. An astute mathematician, Descartes purposed to systematically doubt everything before him unless it was so clear and distinct, or self-evident, that it could not be doubted. From there, he believed, he could rebuild the world with a new system of knowledge and deductions that would lead from despair to a utopia of certainty.

For the process of doubting everything, Descartes applied his skeptical method to the physical world of his senses and even to himself. How do I even know that I'm here? This could all be a dream. But Descartes concluded that there was one crucial piece that could not be doubted, and that was his own doubting. If you are doubting, then a thinker exists. Thus, "I think, therefore I am" (*Cogito ergo sum*). This cogitator (the self) thus became Descartes's new bedrock of what was certain and knowable.

Descartes went and gave thanks to God in a chapel after he arrived at this methodology of "doubting everything but himself," assuming he could rebuild certainty all the way up to belief in God and save humanity's future. The problem was that he effectively hollowed out a "Cartesian pit" from which he could not lift himself, a dualistic separation that echoed the thoughts of Plato. The inner mind and soul are good, while the body and external world are bad, or at least untrustworthy. While Descartes may have been convinced by his own imperfections that a perfect being—namely, God—ought to exist, other thinkers and writers came away with different conclusions. Truth was no longer in the objective world around us; instead the person, the subject, became the arbiter of what was true.

We've all inherited this Cartesian way of seeing the world. It's part of the air we breathe and it's one of the most fundamental pieces to grasp in order to understand how we arrived at our current time of confusion. For if I can doubt everything but my thinking mind, and if everything outside me must conform to my inner world in order to be true, then it's no surprise that we're in a state of widespread anxiety, nihilism, and gender dysphoria.

Remember how easy it is for us to judge all these matters from our contemporary historical bias, hundreds of years after the fact. Luther was trying to do the right thing, as he saw it; Descartes also believed that he would rebuild common faith in God. Whether we champion the ascendency of secular reason and its technological breakthroughs or we mourn the loss of a sacramental worldview that recognized the value of a civilization built upon belief in God, remember that history is always incredibly more nuanced than the simplified versions we've been taught (and what I am presenting here).

We can take the balanced view of the Catholic "both/and," holding the losses and wins in tension, testing everything and holding fast to what is true (see 1 Thessalonians 5:21).

✠ ✠ ✠

Other philosophers built on the legacy of Descartes's *Cogtio ergo sum*, offering a myriad of responses but all pushing the modern hope of "progress" forward. Francis Bacon (1561–1626) emphasized the need for empirical sciences to be further cut off from the abstractions of philosophers; he disagreed with Socrates's belief that knowledge was about growing in virtue, asserting instead that knowledge was about gaining power. Thomas Hobbes (1588–1679), who lived during troubled times in England and became well known for his political philosophies, believed that life is "nasty, brutish, and short" and that humanity needs social contracts through governing states — really, a kind of dictatorship — to keep from tearing itself apart. Jean-Jacques Rousseau (1712–1778) took almost the opposite view. He posited that "natural man" was simple and free, but that "society" (and its effects, such as property and wealth) is the reason for humanity's misery and chains.

Consider the gargantuan technological leap made during these modern centuries. These men saw the invention of the printing press, the steam engine, the telegraph, and the telephone; the mastery of electricity; the introduction of mass production of textiles, new civil engineering tactics, and medical vaccinations; and advances in understanding of genetics. With such technological progress, the idea that humanity could utterly *control* nature (including human nature) seemed well within the realm of possibility.

The nineteenth century saw the thought of figures such as Charles Darwin (1809–1882) and Sigmund Freud (1856–1939) become dominant. Darwin's theory that life is a result of evolution rather than direct, divine creation scandalized many but simultaneously reflected the conclusions the modern philosophers had already posited. *If* God existed, He was a probably a distant clockmaker outside the universe who wound up the cosmos and then checked out (a concept called Deism, which was held by many of America's Founding Fathers). As Darwin's theory spread, it became increasingly in vogue to question if God even existed, for the natural world and its processes could be explained without needing a First Mover involved at all.

Many of us know Freud as the father of psychoanalytic theory. Freud posited that sex and pleasure were key to human happiness. Quite far removed from the likcs of Aristotle and Aquinas's contention that happiness is found in pursuing a virtuous life, Freud believed that a happy life is one where pain is avoided and pleasure indulged.[10] Human flourishing is thus synonymous with sexual pleasure. Any morality that has preceded us is simply a matter of cultural taste with no objective standard; we should thus be free to pleasure ourselves however we see fit. These ideas would have considerable ramifications in the twentieth century and beyond, as many of us today are well aware. Little surprise that Freud disapproved of Christianity.

And so, the philosophers of modernity emphasized the physical and observable world over the invisible or spiritual, and insisted that reason alone would be sufficient to discover ultimate truth. A rediscovered Athens had broken off from Jerusalem and was free of its "chains" to God. Philosophy and theology would remain in their distinct spheres, politely looking across the room at one another. Reason alone would now guarantee the forthcoming utopia here on earth.

What could go wrong?

[10] Sigmund Freud, *Civilization and Its Discontents*, trans. James Strachey (New York: W. W. Norton, 1989), 56.

Nietzsche: "God is Dead, and We Have Killed Him"

Now, a quick examination of the (in)famous Nietzsche. If a person knows of any philosopher aside from the "Big Three" of ancient Greece, it's probably this man. Friedrich Nietzsche (1844–1900) is a polarizing personality who has found a home in pop psychology and trendy college coffee shops. He's either demonized wholesale or seen as a sort of cultural hero. The basic question of his work could be described this way: In a meaningless world, what possible life could be worth living?[11]

I remember a priest-professor of mine who called on our class to take Nietzsche seriously. "Look at him like you would a secular John the Baptist—a prophet *trying* to wake others up to the world he was seeing. But a destructive prophet, to be sure."

Nietzsche grew up in a family of Christian faith, but he avowed that life is ultimately meaningless and without purpose. What's more, he said we should embrace that reality. *Nihilism*, a philosophy which asserts that the universe is utterly devoid of meaning, looks to Nietzsche as one of its heroes. Nietzsche has become a "trendy" philosopher. It's easy to sprinkle his quotes here and there, especially if one has an ax to grind against Christianity or the Western classical tradition. But to take him seriously and live according to his philosophy is to commit oneself to staring into an abyss.

Nietzsche's father died when he was four and he was raised in a household of women. His health was always fragile, forcing him to resign from teaching in his thirties. He wandered around Europe for the remainder of his days. He contracted syphilis,

[11] Norman Melchert, *The Great Conversation*, vol. 2, *Descartes through Derrida and Quine* (New York: Oxford University Press, 2007), 534.

which drove him insane; he died of this terrible disease at the age of fifty-five. While his was a life lived in remarkable pain, his legacy has been one of renown. Among his most famous disciples was Adolph Hitler, who gifted Mussolini a collection of Nietzsche's works when they met.[12] Hitler's belief in the superiority of the Aryan race was encouraged by his reading of Nietzsche, especially the philosopher's disdain for Christianity, which Nietzsche despised in part for its Jewish roots. Hitler relished Nietzsche's call to become an *Übermensch* ("superman"), forcing one's own will upon the weak of society, and his assertion that the "will to power" must reign supreme.

His writing is deliberately provocative and shocking. His infamous assertion that "God is dead" in *The Gay Science* is followed by the almost sorrowful, "God remains dead. *We have killed him*—you and I." Don't interpret this as a declaration of atheism, as many interpret it, but as a prophetic observation that the people of Europe no longer live as if God existed or mattered. The so-called death of God has left Western man adrift in the world. With both widespread belief in God and church attendance crumbling in the twenty-first century, along with the rise in anxiety among people who believe that life has no purpose or guiding telos, Nietzsche has proved to be something of a dark prophet.

Nietzsche didn't care to follow the rules of reason set by Socrates so long ago. He asserted that life is ultimately unreasonable and is thus all about *power*; that the intellect is to be used to wield words as weapons for the sake of gaining power rather than as an instrument to pursue an external, objective truth.

12 Peter Kreeft, *Socrates' Children,* vol. 4, *Contemporary Philosophers* (Elk Grove Village, IL: Word on Fire Institute, 2023), 27.

"What, then, is truth? A mobile army of metaphors, metonyms, and anthropomorphisms ... truths are illusions of which one has forgotten that this is what they are," Nietzsche wrote, "coins which have lost their pictures and now matter only as metal, no longer as coins."[13] He asserted that all knowledge is simply one's perspective, opinion, or interpretation. Things only have value in this world to the extent we give them value—if there's even a *thing* there to begin with. And thus he calls us to become the architects of our own existence

For the reasons above, Nietzsche is often seen as a sort of bridge from the end of the period of modern philosophy to the beginning of a new era, something that will come to be denoted "postmodern" for its new focuses, values, and emphasis. This next period saw the fruit of Nietzsche's observations on full display in the horror of technology turned against humanity in the course of two world wars.

[13] Friedrich Nietzsche, *The Portable Nietzsche*, ed. and trans. Walter Kaufmann (New York: Penguin, 1976), 46–47.

Chapter 6

The Postmoderns

THE MOVEMENT FROM the nineteenth to the twentieth century was fraught with change just as the turn from the medieval to the modern period five hundred years prior. Old dynasties and monarchies such as the Hapsburgs and Romanovs collapsed or were violently overthrown. Technologies that boggled the mind continued to be developed: consider that from 1900 to 1910, the following were invented: the escalator, air conditioning, the tractor, sonar, color photography, the Model T automobile, and the first talking moving picture. Einstein proposed his theory of relativity, and British social theorist Herbert Spencer boldly reinterpreted Darwin's theories into an assumption of unending human progress, asserting that mankind was on the cusp of "human perfectibility," a belief imbibed by the majority of the Western world.

This great "Myth of Progress" captivated the minds of Western leaders, scientists, politicians, preachers, and educators. Atheist-turned-Christian C. S. Lewis wrote, "I grew up believing in this Myth and I have felt—I still feel—its almost perfect grandeur."[14] Applying this technological expertise even to perfecting the human person, Francis Galton coined the word *eugenics*

[14] C. S. Lewis, *Essay Collection: Faith, Christianity and the Church*, ed. Lesley Walmsley (London: HarperCollins, 2000), 26.

(Greek for "good birth") and urged society to subject itself to manipulation to produce the "fittest" population. "What Nature does blindly, slowly, ruthlessly, man may do providently, quickly, and kindly," he declared. "As it lies within his power, so it becomes his duty to work in that direction."[15] Intellectual elites across Europe and the United States began to believe in the promise of a purified human race and rushed into experiments with genetic engineering (and forced sterilizations for the "unfit").

The triumph of technology and unbridled reason seemingly put the nail in the coffin of humanity's need for faith or belief in any God (bringing Nietzsche's prophecies utterly to life).

And then came the First World War and its carnage: mustard gas, machine guns, trench warfare, and the scourging of the European continent. Then the Great Depression that plunged industrialized economies downward for ten years straight. And soon after, the Second World War, with its concentration camps, the fruit of the "racial purity" movement and its horrors, and the dropping of atomic bombs on Japan. The Myth of Progress, the belief that humanity was on a never-ending track of ascendancy toward human perfection thanks to the blessing of technology and reason unfettered by morality or God, was soundly and irrevocably shattered.

The promises of modernity had failed. "Enlightened," "rational" man had committed the greatest evils ever unleashed upon the world.

✠ ✠ ✠

Postmodernism emerged in the wake of this early twentieth-century mayhem as largely a *reaction* to modernism, and it critiqued all

[15] Francis Galton, "Eugenics as a Factor in Religion," in *Essays in Eugenics* (London: Eugenics Education Society, 1909).

previously held values about progress. Its effects can be seen in everything from art and architecture through education and how we even now view our masculine and feminine bodies. The second portion of this book will break open in more detail some of the major thinkers and their theories.

There's no simple set of postmodern principles or a unifying vision by which we can categorize the postmodern mission. If anything, the unifying vision is one of *disunity*: confusion, contradiction, irony, profaning the sacred, and questioning all that has come before.

Author and professor Abigail Favale concisely sums up this contemporary lens as follows:

> Postmodernism, to put it simply, is a worldview that sees reality in terms of narratives that are created by human beings, rather than an order of objective truths that can be discovered by human beings. Postmodernism reflects a deep skepticism toward "metanarratives"—collective, explanatory narratives that give an overarching account of reality.[16]

This skepticism cuts against both traditional religion (such as Christianity and Islam) and "new religions" such as scientism, the belief that science alone can render truth about the world and reality. Devotees of scientism will tell you to "trust the science" or that "the science is settled," as though it were a force or even a person, a benevolent god. "Postmodernists don't necessarily reject the existence of God," Favale continues, "but they do reject the knowability

[16] Abigail Favale, *The Genesis of Gender: A Christian Theory* (San Francisco: Ignatius Press, 2022), 22.

of God and objective truth. . . . God is merely a projection of human desires, a story we tell ourselves."[17]

This new postmodern period has been built, in part, upon the legacy of Plato and Descartes—in particular, the splitting of our body and soul. The advances of modern technology giving us the illusion of control over all of nature, linked with the horror of widespread war and the collapse of institutional trust (governments, churches, and communities), has led to widespread disenchantment. When faced with the many wonders of life on earth and questions about eternity, the only response we can muster is an indifferent "Meh."

We don't know any better, because this is the system we were born into. For instance, many of us were educated in a school setting where our day consisted of being herded from one classroom to the next after set intervals of work, all dictated by the ringing of a bell—much like a factory. The focus of our education was hardly about becoming more *human* (which would require more time devoted to *human*ities: literature, art, philosophy, and the like) or even about being formed into virtuous citizens capable of self-control. School seemed to be more about regurgitating facts in order to pass a test, learning only what was "useful" (maximizing STEM), conforming to the expectations of our peers to find an identity apart from our family, and "jumping through the hoops" of standardized tests in order to climb the next educational rung of the ladder for the sake of joining the labor force.

For this utility-minded model of education, we can thank the American philosopher John Dewey (1859–1952). Dewey lived through every great conflict from the Civil War up through the Korean War. He witnessed the vast changes in life and technology,

[17] Ibid.

and he was heavily influenced by Darwin's naturalistic conception of the world and the human person. He believed that man, like every other animal, is a mere species without a rational soul. He sought to place the works of ancient and medieval scholars firmly in the dustbin of history, keeping only what was "useful" and worthy of "progress." Of these "old ideas" of philosophy, Dewey notes, "We do not solve them: we get over them. Old questions are solved by disappearing, evaporating, while new questions corresponding to the changed attitude of endeavor and preference take their place."[18]

Dewey asserted that we should give up the quest for "certainty," for no certainty is possible in an ever-changing world of fluidity. There is no "higher purpose," and we should stop searching for one. His philosophy was, appropriately, known as *pragmatism.*

Dewey's ideas—or at least the intellectual "mood" he helped to create—influenced Jean-Paul Sartre (1905–1980) and other members of the *existentialist* movement. The existentialists were noted for wrestling with the weight of existence itself. One of Sartre's infamous claims was that "existence precedes essence," meaning that there is no given nature for what constitutes a "human being." We exist first, and then we can make ourselves into what makes us "us."[19] This is yet another addition to Descartes's "I think, therefore I am." We may note a distinct familial resemblance to Ockham's nominalism as well.

The Enlightenment through the Industrial Revolution and into the twentieth century were times fixated on exalting humanity's capacity for unlimited progress and celebrating the inevitable

[18] Melchert, *Great Conversation*, 2:582.

[19] Melchert, *Great Conversation*, 2:648.

achievement of utopia on the horizon. Postmodernity is the cynical, sobered, angry reaction against those broken promises. What is the meaning of life? Nothing! The chickens stirred up by Nietzsche's foreshadowing nihilism have finally come home to roost.

Exported from mostly French intellectuals throughout the mid-1900s to England, Germany, and the United States, "postmodernist doctrines thus drew upon a great deal of philosophical, political, and sociological thought," writes Christopher Butler, "which disseminated itself into the artistic avant-garde (particularly in the visual arts) and into the humanities departments of universities in Europe and the United States as 'theory.'"[20] These ideas were largely skeptical and wielded language not in a search for truth but either in a push to the limits of absurdity or in a grab for power in the "real world."

Angst and absurdity were now in vogue. New belief systems with names like "poststructuralist" or "deconstructionist" flourished. While mostly confined to the halls of academia, these ideas have been spilling over into popular culture over the last several decades and we're now seeing the widespread confusion baked into their formulas.

As in the previous chapters on the eras of philosophical history, let's now take a look at two figures whose thought is continuing to bear its rotten fruit today.

Foucault and Derrida

As in the earlier surveys of philosophical history, it's hard to pin down only *one* thinker as a representative of the entire era. But in the scope of what we are dealing with on the ground as men and

[20] Christopher Butler, *Postmodernism: A Very Short Introduction* (Oxford: Oxford University Press, 2002).

women of the twenty-first century, it's worth spending some time considering the work of two philosophers in particular: Michel Foucault (1926–1984) and Jacques Derrida (1930–2004).

Foucault has been called "Nietzsche's truest twentieth-century successor," as his life quest was one of dismantling the structures around him, including the very foundations of morality.[21] Hating the Catholic education of his youth and feeling liberated by the writings of Marx, Nietzsche, and Freud, Foucault wrote extensively in rejection of Enlightenment values and the promise of modernity. He insisted that there is no common human nature, for we can and should be infinitely malleable, and argued that the idea that history should be understood as an objective quest for a coherent narrative of the past should be abandoned altogether.

Witnessing the California student uprisings of the late 1960s, Foucault became inspired by and fixated on the theme of "power," centering it as the unifying theme undergirding all humanity's activities. Echoing Nietzsche's "will to power," he declared that history itself is a myth. It's all about power, and history attempts to domesticate and control the past in order to validate present structures.[22] "Truth is a thing of this world: it is produced," he said. "Each society has its own regime of truth."[23] (If you've been wondering why, exactly, it's so *en vogue* to be suspicious toward or deride our unifying historical narratives and national heroes, Foucault is largely to blame.)

[21] Merold Westphal, *Suspicion and Faith: The Religious Uses of Modern Atheism* (Grand Rapids, MI: Eerdmans, 1993), 241.

[22] H. D. Harootunian, "Foucault, Genealogy, History: The Pursuit of Otherness," in *After Foucault: Culture, Theory, and Criticism in the 21st Century*, ed. Jonathan Arac (New Brunswick, New Jersey: Rutgers University Press, 1988), 110–137.

[23] Michel Foucault, "Truth and Power," in *Power/Knowledge*, trans. and ed. Colin Gordon (New York: Pantheon, 1980), 131.

Jacques Derrida, born a Sephardic Jew in Algeria, moved to France and studied philosophy. Hopping firmly onto the postmodern train, Derrida desired to undermine everything prior, all the way back to Plato. He attacked everything that is "pure," wanting to turn language itself inside out, beginning with literary texts but eventually subverting all structures.

"There is nothing outside of the text," he infamously posited. Therefore, there is no "true or false." There's only the interpretation we give to something. (This is the final evolution of Ockham's nominalism, by the way: the view that the thing before us is only the name we give it.) While there is a sly, playful, and ironic element to the methodology of Derrida's "deconstruction," there would be deadly consequences once it entered the zeitgeist. A relativistic outlook naturally ensues once a person follows Derrida's thought-line that there is no greater meaning to or Author of the human story.

Attempting to read Derrida's writings is indeed a slog. Peter Kreeft tips his hat to Derrida for "writing the most remarkably unreadable prose in the history of philosophy," and he simply "cannot do justice to deconstructionism because according to deconstructionism itself, justice is impossible; in fact, justice is injustice."[24]

Postmodernity—the era we're currently living in—is simply, as my students used to describe their own sloppy homework assignments, "a hot mess." I use that as a soft term of endearment, however. *This* is the time we have been given by God. *These* are the cultural waters we're all swimming in. It is the mission field God has entrusted to us, whether we asked for it or not; He has placed us here for "such a time as this" (Esther 4:14, NRSVCE). As such, we must seek to understand it in order to find what is lovable and point others toward what is good and true and beautiful.

[24] Kreeft, *Socrates' Children*, 4:280.

Our contemporary era is a unique smoothie of slogans, incoherent mottos, clickbait, and widespread confusion over what makes us fundamentally human. Descartes thought he was going to build a new objective certainty for all things on the foundation of "the self"; today we are reaping the chaotic harvest as every Self is itself a god to be worshiped and beholden to no one. For many of us, there is a palpable sense of ennui and indifference, even decadent rejoicing, as the ship of Western civilization seems to be sinking rapidly, taking on more water with each passing year.

Welcome to the postmodern predicament.

"Why does anyone *believe* these guys?" one of my students asked in exasperation.

We were talking about David Hume in this particular class, a Scottish Enlightenment philosopher who took Descartes's methodology of doubt to its natural end. Noting the lack of certainty we have about life in general, Hume observed that we don't even have a *guarantee* that the sun will rise tomorrow! "That the sun will not rise tomorrow is no less intelligible a proposition, and implies no more contradiction than the affirmation, that it will rise," he wrote. Just because it's risen for the past thirty-three million days in a row, doesn't mean we can know with *certainty* that we shall see it tomorrow!

"That's ridiculous," said another student.

"What kind of way is that to live, Mr. Angel?" asked another.

"How do *these guys* change the world?" yet another asked.

We hadn't even arrived at the postmodern absurdists yet. I've learned, however, that sometimes it takes the absurd to wake up apathetic high school seniors—or grown-ups. Like the proverbial frogs in boiling water, we all can be sucked in by the comforts of our culture and technological blessings, assuming this is "how it's always been" and never ask if we aren't staring at the shadows on the walls of a cave ourselves.

Asking questions is scary. It can also be risky. We risk arriving at information we'd rather not know or upsetting the comfortable status quo over which we feel some measure of control. But every maturing man and woman must ask questions to probe and discern what is true. Am I being told the truth? How can I learn from the minds who went before me?

These are not fun questions to ask because there is a risk. What if everything I thought I knew thus far is false? What if I haven't been given the truth by my teachers, my parents, my government, or the media? Ignorance is bliss, and a pursuit of truth can have dangerous consequences for our comfort. But I cast my lot with Socrates, for the "unexamined life" is truly not worth living.

There were a host of philosophers I wasn't able to name in this first section of the book. Some will appear later, and others I hope you will dive into later in your quest for knowledge. For now, this survey of the history of philosophy is enough to set the scene to understand *how* we arrived at a time in which the basic foundations of human biology and happiness are being shoved aside and the notion of a common truth to strive for is seen as quaint, unenlightened, or even "oppressive." It's now every man for himself.

Interestingly, a number of academics and artists insist that we've already moved into "post-postmodernity." Perhaps. Perhaps that's true in certain faculty lounges or art galleries. But the majority of us are living with the fallout of the ideas that have taken root, from movies and media to policies and procedures. And those are the areas of focus we'll examine next.

Part 2

The Mess

Chapter 7

Abstract Art and Architecture

One of my favorite ways to introduce philosophy to my students and to demonstrate the reality that ideas have consequences was to simply show pieces of art and architecture from five hundred years ago (or longer) and contrast them with pieces from today.

Even the most lethargic of high schoolers could see that beyond the mere passage of time, *something* happened between the Renaissance and our contemporary era. Consider even this short contrasting list of paintings: Michelangelo's *Creation of Adam* in the Sistine Chapel versus the 1962 *Soup Cans* of Andy Warhol; *The Calling of Saint Matthew* by Caravaggio versus the melting clocks of Salvador Dali's *The Persistence of Memory*; or Leonardo da Vinci's *Mona Lisa* versus Edvard Munch's *The Scream.*

Something happened.

How about architecture? A person could walk around New York City, the streets of Cologne, or the gardens of Tokyo and see not just mere design changes due to shifting historical fads and fashions, but also that something *more* occurred over the last centuries. The beliefs about the human person and perspectives that underlie our societies have changed, and our buildings reflect this.

What we value is manifest in our architecture.

Museums used to look majestic and dignified, like the Moscow State Historical Museum or the Kunsthistorisches Museum in Austria. Now we have concrete atrocities like the U.S. Department of Education building in Washington, D.C., or the disorienting Museum of Pop Culture (MoPOP) in Seattle, Washington. Contrast the timeless regality of Buckingham Palace against the dismal J. Edgar Hoover Building that houses the FBI. Even urban flourishes like fencing, benches, water fountains, drainpipes, and parks have all radically changed. We've gone from the lampposts of a novel by Dickens or Conan Doyle to the cold utilitarian streetlights of the suburbs and freeways.

Something happened.

Church buildings are not exempt from this deadening effect in architecture, and they have suffered over the last century. The Gothic cathedrals of yore stand in stark contrast to the sixties and seventies modernist takeover that featured new carpeting, glass and steel beams, blocky abstract art, and the "Resurrected Jesus" who floated out from the Cross. Many Protestant and Catholic worship buildings today look like generic auditoriums with all the latest in audio and visual capacities to compete with the venue of a rock concert but next to nothing to remind a visitor of the sacred dimension of its purpose.

Something happened.

The War on Art

Here's a rather rudimentary but also befuddling question: What is the *point* of art in the first place? What is its purpose? Is a building merely walls and a roof, and therefore we need not worry about any other architectural flourishing? Is a lamppost just a means of illuminating a road or sidewalk? Does a painting exist solely to break up the monotony of a drab, white wall?

Does aesthetics even have a purpose?

Art, properly speaking, is indeed *useless*; that is, it cannot be *used*. Works of art, poetry, and music are not *useful* in the same way a hammer, a car, and a stove are useful. Architecture, likewise, could be understood as a shell in need of no excessive decorative elements—a door or two, walls, a few windows, and a roof are all one *needs* to construct a basic building that functions and provides shelter.

After the Communist takeover of Russia, the new Soviet authorities began experimenting with a "socialist realism" that favored simple geometric shapes, drab colors, and the lack of any decorative flourishes. This evolved into the brutalist movement, which quickly gained favor among the Western cultural elite. A goal of brutalism was to "let brick be brick," let steel be steel, let concrete be concrete. Utilized in thousands of civic buildings and high-rise apartments, the concrete-and-steel structures were hated by the public for their cold, soulless, and overpowering effect on the humans who inhabited their spaces.

In the brutalist school, function took absolute precedence over form, and similarly hideous buildings still exist even across the Western world today. Public-opinion polls consistently show that brutalism is hated by the people, and yet somehow brutalist buildings keep getting built.

A person's *humanity* couldn't flourish in such a brutal environment. But there's still a continual onslaught against the senses happening today in cities of never-ending glass, concrete, and neon emitting its sickly glow in thick, polluted air, with slogans and billboards clouding up every sightline and concrete sprawling as far as the eye can see.

"I felt like destroying something beautiful," Edward Norton's character utters in the 1999 film *Fight Club* after he beats a handsome novice to a pulp. It's a most Nietzschean phrase, one that encapsulates the fight against a shallow, consumeristic, domesticated, and godless existence. There is a desire in our age to spoil beauty. I imagine the impulse to use, tarnish, and destroy is as old as sin and the story of Cain and Abel. But there's a conscious, twisted excitement today to display what is shocking, "pushing the boundaries" as if what is edgy equates to what is true. There's a romantic allure to righteous destruction, regardless of the consequences.

It's why "modern art" is such a joke to so many today. It's also why many young people who have grown up in ugly buildings with disorienting art are starving for beauty and tradition.

Beauty Matters

The first time I watched the 2009 documentary *Why Beauty Matters* by Sir Roger Scruton, it left a profound mark on me. Scruton takes the viewer on a tour of artworks and architecture, allowing the brutalist and absurdist movements within the postmodern art scene to speak for themselves. A "cult of ugliness" has taken over with the goal of shock and effect of widespread banality, which reveals the nihilistic philosophies underneath many of these postmodern movements.

The postmodern take on art often means a mixture of "high" and "low" culture—a delineation which is, itself, purely modern. Many of Mozart's operas, such as the *Magic Flute*, were written as popular entertainment. So, too, were the plays of Shakespeare. Modern artists almost always begin with the condescending assumption that "normal people" have no taste for art. This is absolutely wrong. They simply have no taste for the hideous, perverse objects which now pass for art. The more that artists scorn the public, the uglier their "art" becomes; the uglier their art becomes, the more they're rejected by the public; and so on.

In a 1943 address to the House of Lords, Winston Churchill called for England's bombed-out cities to be rebuilt just as they were before, asserting that, "we shape our buildings and afterwards our buildings shape us." Art and architecture aren't mere flourishes: they inform us about our dignity (or convey a lack thereof). Beautiful works arrest us and stop us in our tracks. The ugly, whether we realize it or not, diminishes and impoverishes the human spirit. Flattened beauty flattens ourselves.

Electric Man

I would conjecture that it's not solely the ideas of philosophers that change the world, but that there is a symbiotic relationship with the developments in technology that make new ideas fashionable or believable. Many of the ideas undergirding deconstruction, for instance, would not be gripping our young people today if not for social media platforms.

The technology that allows us to stall or circumvent the conception of a child, for instance, leads us to believe that we are the true authors and arbiters of human life. The capability to inject hormones and surgically amputate fully functioning body parts makes us think that we could actually change our sex to become whatever we wish: male, female, or an androgynous hybrid.

"Electric man has no bodily being. He is literally dis-carnate," wrote Canadian philosopher and media analyst (and Catholic convert) Marshall McLuhan, "which is a tremendous menace to an incarnate Church."[25] We live in a landscape of never-ending screens and light, at once entrancing and dehumanizing. It has been a thrilling and relentless march over the last century: radio to TV to computers to the Internet to the smartphone to AI. We adopt these technologies without any ethical framework of how to use them correctly. We mediate nature and moments of tenderness through screens, ready to whip out a cellphone to "capture" a moment rather than staying present to it—"digital contraception," a mentor of mine called it.

I remember one year when our school administration encouraged students to use digital textbooks on school-issued iPads. Most teachers were fine with it, except for our theology department, which (rightly) rebelled. We foresaw the behavioral problems that would ensue when the device that is their theology textbook is also their gaming machine. I taught freshmen at that time and even my best students couldn't handle the temptation to swipe from lecture notes to Fortnite. The experiment lasted for one year before the administration rolled back the policy.

There's great fascination around the succession of generations, as we pass the baton from boomers to Gen X, from Gen X to millennials, and from millennials to Zoomers. We tease each other. We blame each other for society's woes. There's also great concern about generational cycles in history, which supposedly doom us to repeat the mistakes of our ancestors. These theories can inspire hopelessness or excitement, depending on our outlook on life. Many have theorized that it is "major events" that can mark, bond, or change one generation to the next, such as World War II for the

[25] Marshall McLuhan, *The Medium and the Light: Reflections on Religion* (Eugene, OR: Wipf and Stock, 2010), 50.

Greatest Generation, 9/11 for millennials or the COVID-19 pandemic for Gen Z.

Jean Twenge, acclaimed author of *iGen*, puts forth the argument in her subsequent work *Generations* that it's actually *technology* and the tools we use that have the greatest impact on shifting one epoch of humanity to the next. "Our lives are strikingly different from the lives of those in decades past, primarily due to the technology we rely on," Twenge writes, noting:

> Technological change isn't just about stuff; it's about how we live, which influences how we think, feel, and behave.... While hunter-gatherers lived in small groups, agriculture led to larger towns and eventually complex societies that required more structure and cooperation. In more recent times, certain technological developments have ultimately led to behavioral and attitude changes far beyond the device itself.[26]

Looking around, this makes sense. We can certainly say that the increased availability of information does not mean we have become wiser. Now we're rapidly entering the strange new world of artificial intelligence advancing by leaps and bounds every year, having dramatic consequences for a variety of industries and career fields. We are becoming faster processors of information, but with dwindling attention spans and capacities for memories.

In reducing our daily stress load through all our modern conveniences, a counterintuitive effect occurs that can lead to

[26] Jean M. Twenge, *Generations: The Real Differences Between Gen Z, Millennials, Gen X, Boomers, and Silents—and What They Mean for America's Future* (New York: Atria Books, 2023), 14.

increases in chronic stress. We know that the consumption of ultra-processed, genetically-modified food disrupts our microbiomes, yet it's so cheap and abundantly available that we eat it anyway. We become prisoners of our own appetites. Regular exposure to heat and cold and daily movement and exercise promote gene expression and adaptability, but in an age where we can move from one air-conditioned bubble to the next, why bother embracing discomfort? We never turn off our devices, fixated as we are on scrolling and trying to "optimize" or "hack" every facet of life. And we're continually left more exhausted in the process.

Much ink has been spilled on how technology has led to the atomization of ourselves. We can exist in our own little bubbles and do not need to rub up against the "inconveniences" imposed by interacting with other people. Yet, by insulating ourselves from others, we paradoxically diminish ourselves. With an "every man for himself" mentality, we come away with less. Philosopher Charles Taylor has written extensively on the shift from a communal mentality to an individualistic one. He speaks of "the loss of a heroic dimension to life":

> People no longer have a sense of a higher purpose, of something worth dying for. Alexis de Tocqueville sometimes talked like this in the last century, referring to the "petits et vulgaires plaisirs"[27] that people tend to seek in the democratic age. In another articulation, we suffer from a lack of passion. Kierkegaard saw "the present age" in these terms. And Nietzsche's "last men" are

[27] "Petty and vulgar phrases."

> at the final nadir of this decline; they have no aspiration left in life but to a "pitiable comfort."[28]

Taylor astutely observes that "the dark side of individualism is a centering on the self, which both flattens and narrows our lives, makes them poorer in meaning, and less concerned with others or society."[29] Enclosed within our cares and numbed by the soft glow of ever-present screens, the longer-term consequences are manifesting themselves more with each passing year.

Starved for beauty and numbed by comfort. This is where we find ourselves today.

[28] Charles Taylor, *The Malaise of Modernity* (1991; repr., Toronto: House of Anansi Press, 2003), 12.

[29] Ibid.

Chapter 8

Everything Is Marxist

"Oh, *everything* is 'Marxist,' now, huh?" a college student flippantly commented to me once, dismissing the meta-point I was trying to make in our conversation.

I simply shrugged. "Well, yeah … at some level, everything *is* Marxist now." Put Nietzsche and Marx in a blender, and you've got the soil for just about every cultural movement budding today. (The conversation didn't end well).

From tense race relations to the politicization of the climate to the confusion surrounding even what it means to be a woman or a man—all of this *is* a fruit of the Marxist tree which has its roots spread through the subterrane of Western thought.

Philosophy professor Stephen Hicks illustrates how we arrived at this quagmire in his insightful and engaging commentary *Explaining Postmodernism*. Hicks explains how Marxism began as a framework for achieving an atheistic, egalitarian utopia. Over time, however, its basic "oppressor versus oppressed" premise has been adapted to each new cultural moment. The echoes of this system of thought seem to haunt the halls of seemingly every institution and agency today.

It's worth a quick detour to pause and examine who exactly Karl Marx was and why his thought still lingers with us today.

Marx 101

Let's take a brief, perhaps sympathetic, look at Marx, the world he inhabited, and what he was trying to achieve.

Karl Marx was born in Germany in 1818. As a young man he witnessed the inhuman working conditions and negligible wages of the factory workers of his time, and it (rightly) left a poor taste in his mouth. He grew to despise unbridled capitalism (and religion as well). That laborers offered their services for any wage at all offended Marx, and he, with his partner, friend, and financier Friedrich Engels, published *The Communist Manifesto* at the same time revolutions were breaking out all over Europe, destabilizing established monarchies like those in France, Hungary, and Denmark. "Let the ruling classes tremble at a Communistic revolution," they wrote. "The proletarians have nothing to lose but their chains."[30]

The desired uprising from the working class and the overthrow of the world order never fully materialized, though. Marx himself was kicked out of several countries and died in England a stateless person. His family was ravaged by debt, depression, and multiple suicides.

A tree is known by its fruit, though, and the body count for nations espousing a Marxist worldview is high indeed. Marx and Engels remarked that "Communism abolishes eternal truths, it abolishes all religion, and all morality."[31] The *Black Book of Communism*, a 1997 work compiled by an international group of academics, concluded that the human cost of genocides,

[30] Karl Marx and Friedrich Engels, *Manifesto of the Communist Party*, 1848, chap. 4, Marxists Internet Archive, https://www.marxists.org/archive/marx/works/1848/communist-manifesto/ch04.htm.

[31] Ibid., chap. 2, https://www.marxists.org/archive/marx/works/1848/communist-manifesto/ch02.htm.

executions, deportations, and famines under Marxist governments (the foremost being China, the Soviet Union, and Cambodia), stood at over 94 million.[32] A small price to pay for utopia, some would say. "To put it brutally, you can't make an omelette without breaking eggs," noted Stalin sympathizer Walter Duranty of the *New York Times* in 1933.

The Morphing of Marxism

Now, postmodernism is not *synonymous* with Marxism, nor do postmodern thinkers inherently, by some default setting, adhere to Marxist beliefs. Not every "deconstructionist" philosopher, brutalist architect, or Lacanian psychoanalyst is necessarily a Marxist.

However, Marxism *is* largely baked into the batter of many layers of postmodern thought. If nothing else, it is because men and women existing in a desert of objective truth need *some* system of belief to hang their hat on. In a culture devoid of any moral standards due to the rejection of divine commandments and natural law, the Marxist lens of oppressor versus oppressed at least provides some paradigm by which we can make sense of the world.

"The first postmodernists were reacting largely to the failure of Marxism, the longstanding analytical framework of the academic left, and suffering from major disillusionment," Helen Pluckrose and James Lindsay note in their thorough work *Cynical Theories*. "Because their theoretical framework of choice was falling apart, they adopted the cynical attitude that nothing could be relied upon anymore. … So, by the 1990s, the applied

[32] Stéphane Courtois, et al., *The Black Book of Communism: Crimes, Terror, Repression*, trans. Jonathan Murphy and Mark Kramer (Cambridge, MA: Harvard University Press, 1999).

postmodern turn had arrived, made postmodern Theory actionable, and focused on identity and identity politics."[33]

Within this paradigm, all of life comes down to a game of power—who's "on top" and who should be dethroned. Marx's school of thought within sociology, also called Conflict Theory, was taken up by scholars of the so-called "Frankfurt School" in the early 1900s, who developed "Critical Theory," which aimed at the social and structural transformation of society. From this tree, we now have the fruit of "Critical Legal Studies": "Critical Race Theory" and its growing number of offshoots.

These theories are worldviews masquerading as analytic tools, and they are interested not in reform or reconciliation but *revolution*. Objective truth isn't a pursuit of critical theories either, so good luck trying to hold its feet to the fire. "An approach based on critical theory calls into question the idea that objectivity is desirable or even possible," write Robin DiAngelo and Ozlem Sensoy, two leading critical theorists. "Knowledge is ... reflective of the values and interests of those who produce it."[34] (Remember the postmodern turn to the view that any sort of truth is ultimately unknowable?)

This has taken on new form today in what is often referred to as "intersectionality" (or as "the victim hierarchy" by its opponents), a manner of perceiving all differences as oppressions that peoples (usually minorities) claim to suffer. The word *intersectionality* first came on the scene through Kimberle Crenshaw, a student of Derrick Bell, the father of Critical Race Theory.

[33] Helen Pluckrose and James Lindsay, *Cynical Theories: How Activist Scholarship Made Everything about Race, Gender, and Identity—and Why This Harms Everybody* (Durham, NC, Pitchstone, 2020), 184–185.

[34] Robin DiAngelo and Ozlem Sensoy, *Is Everyone Really Equal? An Introduction to Key Concepts in Social Justice Education*, 2nd ed. (New York: Teachers College Press, 2017), 73, Kindle.

Now, intersectionality possesses a kernel of truth in that we all partake in an intricate web of interactions with other humans that influence our experience of life and our understanding of our humanity. The trouble is that, according to its founder, this worldview is inseparable from feminist ideology, identity politics, and the Marxist notion of life as fundamentally a battle between oppressor and oppressed.[35]

Remember, by the way, that critical theories are *theories* and not facts—and if they state they are *true* or *factual*, then they are refuting the postmodern assertion that truth is unknowable.

In *Explaining Postmodernism,* Hicks illustrates how each subsequent wave of Marxist thought has, after failing to usher in a lasting and final revolution, morphed anew to find its new crusade. Our generation's radical environmentalists, militant multiculturalists, and postmodern academics are the true heirs of the twentieth century's revolutionary socialists, still impatiently waiting to bring about the hoped-for utopia of revolution.

"Anti-racism" is one of the newer concepts on the scene of popular postmodern thought. Of course, being *against racism* is nothing new, and I hope that no one reading this book would need to have the evils of racism explained to them. But when used by modern intellectuals the term *anti-racism* refers to a very specific concept—one that, again, sees racism as a synonym for oppression in the Marxist sense. So, according to anti-racist literature, it's possible for people of darker skin to be "white nationalists" if they support or participate in systems or ideas which (according to anti-racist thinkers) perpetuate the "oppression of nonwhites."

[35] Voddie Baucham Jr., *Fault Lines: The Social Justice Movement and Evangelicalism's Looming Catastrophe* (Washington, DC: Salem Books, 2021), 146–147.

The truth is that all human DNA is 99.9 percent identical. As geneticist Duana Fullwiley writes, "There is no genetic basis for race."[36] Spencer Wells, who headed the joint National Geographic Society-IBM nonprofit Genographic Project, affirmed, "Racism is not only socially divisive, but also scientifically incorrect," for we share virtually the same genome but with variations in skin pigmentation, height, or other adaptations for the sake of our environments.[37] We share in one, common, God-given humanity. Racism obscures this reality. So do the Marxist-infused Critical Theories. Both enshrine and reinforce our differences, and with the same goal: sowing the seeds of hatred and violence.

Clearly, anti-racism is not interested in reconciliation. It explicitly rejects the colorblind society articulated by Dr. Martin Luther King Jr. and his allies. Instead, it seeks to violently destroy the structures of Western civilization, especially the nuclear family, which are said to propagate racism. According to the Critical Theorists, these institutions cannot be salvaged. They exist only to perpetuate white power; indeed, the very concept of "Western civilization" (they say) is inherently racist. And so, it must be destroyed.

The Attack on the Family

One of the most insidious facets of Marxist thought is its desire to dismantle the family. The family as the domestic unit of society, in Marx's teachings, must be subordinated to the priorities of the state. Therefore, the devotion of husband to wife must be broken and

[36] Quoted in "Race in a Genetic World," *Harvard Magazine*, May-June 2008, https://www.harvardmagazine.com/2008/05/race-in-a-genetic-world-html.

[37] Ibid.

both should be sent to work outside the home. Children are understood as a burden and interruption to meaningful work. They should be aborted if they are foreseen to be too great an inconvenience. Otherwise, they too must be sent out of the home to public schools, where the state will raise them up to become the next generation of obedient workers.

The Marxist frame of oppressor versus oppressed pits man against woman, women against her children, children against parents, and so on. When Mao Zedong enacted the Communist Cultural Revolution in the 1960s and 1970s, he targeted China's youth to be "re-educated" into Marxist thought police and impelled many boys and girls to turn against their parents. The same subtle tactics are employed to turn young people, who naturally wrestle with dynamics of peer approval and questions of identity, against their parents and caregivers, entrusting themselves more to teachers and agents of the state.

"We can't destroy the inequalities between men and women until we destroy marriage," wrote one author in the anthology *Sisterhood Is Powerful.*[38] Marxist thought wants nothing to do with the complementary dynamic between man and woman which is given to us by God, and which (of course) is the foundation of the family; therefore, it must stamp out the familial relationship of parents and children as the cell of society and the first school of love.[39]

All these philosophies that stem from Marxism—from Critical Theories to Feminist/Gender Studies programs to Liberation

[38] Robin Morgan, "The Feminists vs. The Institution of Marriage," in *Sisterhood is Powerful: An Anthology of Writings from the Women's Liberation Movement*, ed. Robin Morgan (New York: Random House, 1970), 537.

[39] Trent Horn and Catherine R. Pakaluk, *Can a Catholic Be a Socialist? (The Answer is No—Here's Why)* (El Cajon, CA: Catholic Answers Press, 2019), 93.

Theology movements—have the same virus of Marxist class warfare baked into them. Warning about the rise of Marxist influence in the 1960 and 1970s, Pope St. Paul VI asserted that it would be "illusory and dangerous" to "accept the elements of Marxist analysis without recognizing their relationships with ideology, and to enter into the practice of class struggle and its Marxist interpretations, while failing to note the kind of totalitarian and violent society to which this process leads."[40]

Why the Appeal of Marxism?

Polls continue to show that a majority of millennials and Gen-Zers look at socialism favorably.[41] With such a high death count and low return on investment, why would any person today give credence to the claims of Marxism?

First of all, there's widespread ignorance (especially in America) when it comes to how a Communist political system plays out in reality. We can sit with our smartphones, lattes on demand, and two-day shipping and bemoan the comforts which would have bewildered our forefathers. "The grass is probably greener over there," many imagine, not knowing what true hunger, desperation, and oppression actually feel like. We don't know what it's like to have our property stripped away, to lose the right to worship how we choose, and to have our bread rationed by the state.

[40] Pope Paul VI, Apostolic Letter *Octogesima Adveniens* (May 14, 1971), no. 34, https://www.vatican.va/content/paul-vi/en/apost_letters/documents/hf_p-vi_apl_19710514_octogesima-adveniens.html.

[41] Theodore Bunker, "YouGov Poll: Millennial Majority Would Vote for Socialist," Newsmax, October 28, 2019, https://www.newsmax.com/newsfront/socialism-millennials-capitalism-generation-x/2019/10/28/id/939028/.

We in America have been schooled thoroughly (and rightly) on the evils of Nazism and the horror of the Holocaust, but most history classes neglect to teach the death tolls of the Communist regimes of Russia, China, or Cambodia in the twentieth century. I barely heard a word about Marx or Communism in my own educational journey, unless it was somehow in a lionization of the Russian Revolution or seeing the image of guerilla leader Che Guevara (a murderer who held quite racist views) on college students' t-shirts or the walls of hip coffee shops.

To the extent that millennials and Gen Z witnessed the fallout of the unbridled greed and financial collapse of 2008, many have been left suspicious of the system of capitalism in general. Especially as the cost of living in the West continues to rise and many feel disillusioned by college debt and pessimistic about ever reaching the milestones of their parents, the suspicion and anger continue to simmer. Add into the mix the breakdown of the family and widespread fatherlessness, and it's no wonder that we have a culture that is severely directionless, wounded, and filled with a nameless rage that needs to be directed somewhere.

The call to "save the world" is powerful and it runs deep. Consider the allure to many young boys (like my own past adolescent self) of superheroes and video games that champion the mantras to be a hero, step up to one's mission and endure hardship, and in effect save the world. This very language is utilized all around the climate change debate. To literally save the world, we must compost food and switch to electric vehicles: the planet is at stake. (Now why anyone who espouses a materialist or nihilist ethos should care about perpetuating an ultimately indifferent planet or appeasing some fantasy projection of Gaia or Mother Earth, I have no idea. But this is where we are today.)

People who feel righteous anger at the inequalities in the world often gravitate to Marxist thought in an attempt to right the wrongs of unfettered greed or discrimination. "Organized religion" has largely been written off as part of the problem, so we might as well try Marxism again. The problem is that in socialist thought, "equality" is not a matter of providing people with equal *opportunities*. It's a matter of forcing equal *outcomes*, even if this requires discriminating against others or stealing their property in the process, to level everyone to the same base (except for the chosen overlords, the only ones who can be trusted with managing the wealth of the inept masses). Pope Leo XIII warned against this movement in his 1891 letter *Rerum Novarum*, saying "it is impossible to reduce civil society to one dead level. Socialists may in that intent do their utmost, but all striving against nature is in vain."[42] Leo recognized that, more often than not, socialists' grievances are legitimate. They're angered by real economic and political abuses. The problem is that the *means* by which they seek to redress this injustice are, in themselves, unjust. Their methods do not ameliorate human suffering: they drastically increase it.

Reorienting Ourselves

When we find ourselves lost, one of the first action items should be to orient ourselves back to the right direction. It could be finding the North Star, a river in the woods, or a mile marker or street name.

One of the biggest errors within Marxism is that it simply gets our anthropology (and thus the direction of our lives) wrong. The

[42] Pope Leo XIII, Encyclical Letter on Capital and Labor *Rerum Novarum* (May 15, 1891), no. 17, https://www.vatican.va/content/leo-xiii/en/encyclicals/documents/hf_l-xiii_enc_15051891_rerum-novarum.html.

contemporary framework for understanding the human person—that men and women are merely materialistic creatures who can determine their own meaning through the elimination of God and will always trend toward "progress" with the correct economic system in place that distributes goods equally—is not just incorrect, but it is dangerously wrong. We've seen it again and again.

To the extent that we misunderstand our being, we misread our bearing. Proper social justice means putting ourselves in right order. It means developing healthy relationships with God and our fellow men. "Put first things first and we get second things thrown in," wrote C. S. Lewis in 1951, "put second things first and we lose *both* first and second things."[43]

To the extent we've lost the ordering of a society that even passively respects a Sabbath day and pays lip service to God, it's no wonder that we struggle to get our ducks in a row. "When Sunday loses its fundamental meaning and becomes merely part of a 'weekend,'" wrote St. John Paul II, "it can happen that people stay locked within a horizon so limited that they can no longer see 'the heavens.' Hence, though ready to celebrate, they are really incapable of doing so."[44]

"You always have the poor with you," Jesus affirmed (Mark 14:7, NRSVCE). Christ wasn't rejoicing in this fact. He was simply acknowledging the reality that, on this side of heaven, there will always be material inequality that entails both suffering for men and women worldwide and the invitation for those more

[43] C. S. Lewis to Dom Bede Griffiths, April 23, 1951, in *The Collected Letters of C. S. Lewis*, vol. 3, *Narnia, Cambridge and Joy, 1950–1963,* ed. Walter Hooper (San Francisco: HarperSanFrancisco, 2007), 111.

[44] Pope John Paul II, Apostolic Letter on Keeping the Lord's Day Holy *Dies Domine* (May 31, 1998), no. 4. https://www.vatican.va/content/john-paul-ii/en/apost_letters/1998/documents/hf_jp-ii_apl_05071998_dies-domini.html.

fortunate to be His hands and feet of service. But an invitation to freely give is quite different than the state compelling you to hand over your goods, property, and possessions. Certainly, we all have different gifts and have been dealt different hands in life, but for the Christian this is an opportunity to voluntarily (freely) build up the Body of Christ, not do so forcibly by state mandate.

The socialistic and communistic movements assert that the person exists for the collective state. A proper Catholic, Christian understanding is that the state exists to serve the irreplaceable human person.

Chapter 9

The Deconstructing Deception

This book initially started in my head years ago as I was musing on the popularizing of this word that has trickled out of academia and into the popular zeitgeist—one that we have already touched on, albeit briefly and quite vaguely. The word is *deconstruction.*

It seems harmless, right? Outside of the context of philosophy, one would think that the word refers to knocking apart a building or disassembling a city of LEGO bricks so you can build a new, more ingenious structure. But, as noted earlier, the word philosophically stems from the work of Derrida and his disciples. It comes embedded with a particularly nuanced set of expectations. There is very specific agenda baked into the meaning of the word and it's important for any discerning man or woman to understand what is at stake in employing it.

According to the American Psychological Association, the term *deconstruction* is

> a form of critical analysis of literary texts and philosophical positions that is based on the twin assumptions that there can be no firm referents for

> language and *no adequate grounding for truth claims* [emphasis added]. . . .
>
> A deconstructive reading of a text will generally use traditional analytical methods to expose the innumerable ways in which the text subverts its own claims to meaning and coherence. In much general usage, the term is now taken to be synonymous with the destruction of an idea or a truth claim.[45]

Did you catch that? "No adequate grounding for truth claims."

According to Derrida, the self of a man or a woman is merely another "text" to be deconstructed. *All* reality, from our countries' histories and heroes to our religious beliefs to the very biology of our bodies is merely a "construct" of language and worthy of dismantling.[46]

Language Games

Deconstruction in particular, and the postmodern project in general, is a war on *language*. As language is a vital means of demarking and articulating reality, deconstructing language is often about dismantling reality itself (or at least attempting to) and questioning the foundation of what makes life intelligible and stable. This foundation under attack includes understanding what we value as countries and our national histories, belief in and articulation of the nature of God, and the dignity and complementarity of male and female, as the family is the building block of society.

[45] "Deconstruction," APA Dictionary of Psychology, updated April 19, 2018, https://dictionary.apa.org/deconstruction.

[46] Butler, *Postmodernism*, 21.

Part of what makes any culture coherent is its unifying principles: what it values, the holidays it celebrates, the heroes it upholds. A crucial yet often overlooked aspect of a cohesive culture is its language. If we have groups of people that can't communicate with one another, it's no wonder that confusion and chaos ensue. It's the Tower of Babel all over again.

This is also why there's such a fierce battle over the curious use of someone's "preferred pronouns" today—this compulsion of other people's speech *must* occur in order to override the reality at hand. To acknowledge any external, objective truth runs a risk of collapsing the delicate house of cards that has been constructed. This methodology requires cowing people into submission and forcing people to speak what they often know is fundamentally untrue.

"A student who knows what a subject and a predicate are is much more likely to understand that God's existence can be logically proved," writes Peter Kreeft. By the same principle,

> A student who knows that both human thought and language and the material universe are by their own intrinsic nature rationally structured is not likely to be a skeptic, a subjectivist, a New Ager, or a Deconstructionist. Nietzsche sagely observed that "we atheists have not abolished God until we have abolished grammar." For grammar is the reflection of The Word in words, the reflection of the ordering reason of the Creator in the ordered structure of the creature's language.[47]

[47] Peter Kreeft, "What is Classical Education?" Memoria Press, April 19, 2009, https://www.memoriapress.com/articles/what-is-classical-education/.

Deconstructionism assumes two things. First, there is no good or bad, only one's interpretation. Second, words themselves have no meaning, so "truth" can be whatever I want it to be. "Ye shall be as gods," Satan told Adam and Eve in the Garden, as his first act was to *twist God's words* to suit them to a self-serving purpose (Gen. 3:5, DRA). If the gospel is the "good news," then what better way to muddle the very communication of God's Word (John 1:1) than through "deconstruction."

Jesus declares Himself "the way, and the truth, and the life" (John 14:6, NRSVCE), and we have forever twisted His meaning to be *a* way—that is, one way among many different ways—that's basically optional. He may be His own "truth," but He's not mine. He is only "life" insofar as He does not contradict my own lifestyle.

We're *all* susceptible to this self-centered turn, due to our fallen human nature. We all have something "bent" within us that wants to define life by our own terms. In many ways, the modern fad of deconstruction is a very old error but in new packaging. This wave of deconstructing has been a long time building, and we're now seeing its breakers crash all around us.

War on Reality

In 1917, the Virgin Mary appeared to three small children in Fatima, Portugal. In these apparitions, Mary called for the return to faith in God and lives of prayer, lest a greater war would occur and "the errors of Russia would spread throughout the world."

The Russian Revolution and its ideas, already set in motion, furthered the idea that human nature was malleable and—with Marx as its prophet—society could be violently rearranged into a utopia of equality. But since nature and all that is natural, such as the family, manifests inequality and the objective truth of its nature, "Lenin et al. had to tear it all down," writes Dr. Carrie Gress. "The natural and the supernatural orders were the real obstacles that had to be destroyed."[48] The warnings at Fatima went largely unheeded, and today the errors they decried attack the very root of objective reality.

A key part of reshaping society in the first place was the breakdown of language. George Orwell called it "Newspeak" in his novel *1984*, the propagandistic language that is the inversion of words' true meanings. "Tolerance" today, for instance, doesn't truly mean that all ideas and perspective and backgrounds are welcome at the table; the new definition often implies the uniformity of only *one* acceptable type of perspective, not a true marketplace of plurality and consequence-free exploration of thought. A person's innate maleness or femaleness is now called "sex *assigned* at birth" (sex is thus reframed as *imposed* from the outside, not something objective and inherent in our creation). Even labels like "misinformation" are slapped across videos and articles by the very entities we should inherently distrust for their sheer lack of transparency and ability to tell the truth in the first place.

It's always easier to destroy than to create, easier to tear down than to build up. In the name of relentless autonomy, we destroy any perceived threat to our own selfish freedom. *Revolution* is a seemingly romantic word for our time, and our cultural leaders often whitewash the horrific death tolls of their rampages. A study issued by the University of Mary observes this "strange barbarity" that permeates the progressive vision of society:

[48] Carrie Gress, *The Anti-Mary Exposed: Rescuing the Culture from Toxic Femininity* (Charlotte, NC: TAN Books, 2019), 34.

> Despite its sophistication, its gilded rhetoric, and high hopes for good things, [this vision] has a destructive core. It promises a social and personal paradise, but saddled with a false understanding of humanity and its ills and thinking that the desired utopia will arrive as a matter of course once the requisite restraints have been demolished, it too leaves behind not a lush garden but a howling wasteland.[49]

Christianity Meets Deconstruction

I'd like to turn toward what exactly deconstruction potentially entails for the disciple of Christ. To lay my cards out on the table: the term *deconstruction* makes my eye twitch, especially when Christians use it. I've had my own journey of becoming aware of this term and seeing several young people, former students and their friends, swept away by this trendy concept that seems to lead not only to confusion but to new (though false) freedom, and to the almost-inevitable leaving of Christianity wholesale by those utilizing its methodology.

A few years ago my wife and I filmed a video for YouTube in which I tried to name this problem and sound the warning bell about the threat that this deconstruction fad poses for Christians. The response varied by platform: many on YouTube were appreciative and noted that it helped to clarify some questions, but on other social media there was a deluge of pushback that ranged from disagreement to mockery and contempt. I had stumbled into a minefield of reactions, which demonstrated the truth of my

[49] *From Christendom to Apostolic Mission: Pastoral Strategies for an Apostolic Age* (Bismarck, ND: University of Mary Press, 2020), 87.

claim that these ideas have already taken root. A number of individuals declared that "*My* Jesus would be fine with the way I am living my life," demonstrating the insidious nature of the self-centered *I* that governs under a deconstructive methodology.

I was ready to tangle with ideas, but what I hadn't realized was how many people had equated their *identity* with deconstructionism. This was something new.

There's been an explosion in the Protestant world over the last few decades of those who identify themselves as people who are "deconstructing their faith." Hashtags like "exvangelical" and "ex-christian" and calls to "*decolonize* your theology" abound on social media. For many men and women who have left their faith behind, what pushes them out of any structured Christianity is usually rejection of a literalistic reading of the Bible, objection to teachings around sexual morality, a toxic experience of "female submission" or unhealthy purity culture, and an overidentification with political conservatism (especially after the 2016 election of Donald Trump as president).[50] Many people have been ostracized or labeled "heretics" for simply asking questions about their beliefs.

None of this came out of nowhere. Remember that ideas have consequences. If you look at the work of women and men who approach the task of deconstruction with the (ironic) zeal of an evangelist, you will often see a great deal of heartache. It can sound akin to those who are going through a divorce—hurt, anger, resentment and the outpouring of emotions are often on full display. Many women and men have been abused through the twisting of Scripture to justify manipulating or controlling behaviors. Against such pain and heartbreak, deconstruction is the way that people

50 Alisa Childers and Tim Barnett, *The Deconstruction of Christianity: What it Is, Why It's Destructive, and How to Respond* (Carol Stream, IL: Tyndale Elevate, 2024), 33–34

have been able to give voice to the hurt they have experienced from a distorted Christian upbringing. To try and push back against their claims without listening to the expressions of real pain often leads to a justified recoil of anger.

I think one of the biggest reasons why deconstruction hasn't caught on wholesale within Catholicism the same way it has within Protestantism is because of the nature of *authority*. After the Protestant Reformation, it really was an "every man for himself" mentality, as every person essentially became their own mini-pontiff. Each Christian could decide what was right or wrong, what teachings to believe or reject, and what within the tradition of the Church could be kept or discarded. Without a unifying catechism or official Magisterium to referee disputes or teachings, the situation is ripe for that "it's true for you but not for me" attitude we see everywhere today. That kind of autonomy is intoxicating in our fallen human state, to be sure, but it also leads to the prison cell of the self.

Now there *are* certainly individuals, clergy, and movements urging deconstruction within Catholicism, voices that invite us to revisit the abuses, crimes, and negligences committed by Catholics throughout history and into our own day. And as with socialists, their grievance is often totally valid. Yet, also like socialism, the "solution" is a type of commiserating groupthink, a desire to wallow in the hurt rather than move forward into a place of healing and forgiveness. And there are often bad actors involved who simply have an axe to grind against the Catholic Church and any institution deemed "patriarchal" or possessing "power." Look no further than the continual attack on St. Junípero Serra, the Franciscan friar who revered the indigenous peoples of California and pled for their humane treatment under the Spanish settlers.

There have always been theologians and clerics trying to take the Catholic Church and warp the interpretation of Christ's teachings in a variety of different directions. Since the Second Vatican Council especially there have been a great variety of distorted teachings, incongruent theologies, and wonky forms of liturgical expression. All the more reason to (literally!) thank God for imparting upon the Church the pope as the authoritative head of the Magisterium, which is the official teaching body of the Church that delineates the truth from among the myriad of ways of interpreting the Scriptures. Thank God for St. John Paul II, for instance, and his grand teaching on the goodness of the human body, of being male and female, and the call for spouses to *mutually* submit themselves to one another in love in the imitation of the self-sacrificial love of Christ.

A great number of people who have found meaning or even healing through New Age practices or yoga likewise become extremely defensive if a fellow Christian raises concerns about the congruity of these practices within the framework of living as a disciple of Jesus Christ. Again, to the extent that we have made these practices our *identity*, any critique of a practice or idea feels like a personal attack. The pastoral approach must always be one of being willing to listen and step into the hurt that someone has acknowledged. That pain must be validated, and we all have something to learn from one another.

We already have vocabulary for the process of questioning the Faith or dealing with the doubts that arise from believing in an invisible God and trusting in the Church and the doctrines of the Faith. And every maturing man and woman needs to ask questions of their faith and seek the answers to the hard questions. Only in cults are people shunned for asking questions. Some use the word *deconstruction* as a synonym for this sincere seeking, but that is a misuse of a word that is pre-loaded with its own specific meaning.

Deconstructing at large is not concerned about getting theology right or looking back to the Church Fathers or early councils for wisdom. It's about tearing down doctrines and structures that the individual person disagrees with, aiming not to conform to the gospel but to conform the gospel to the self. That temptation is nothing new. As Archbishop Fulton Sheen would say, it's an "old error with a new label." And if this fad comes out of the mindset of Derrida, who negated belief in any knowable truth, then that way surely lies madness.

Chapter 10

Male and Female We Have Lost Them

One of the most tangible pieces of evidence of the postmodern fallout is the attack on the very essence of what constitutes "male" and "female" today. These categories, once as sturdy and reliable as the rising and setting of the sun, have come under attack as infinitely malleable and without any reasonable anchor in the material world.

As we've seen, so much of the postmodern project's aim is purposeful dismantling where there has been established order. This is no more evident than in the attacks we've witnessed on the essential categories of *man* and *woman*. Because God, natural law, and any notion of design or purpose have been cast aside in our educational institutions, we're left with the mere "will to power" of every individual, defining their reality for themselves.

The Christian thinker Carl Trueman notes that Nietzsche's "death of God" signified a "death of human nature, or at least the end of any cogent argument that there is such a thing as human nature." According to Trueman, "If there is no God, then men and women cannot be made in his image and are not therefore required to act in accordance with that image."[51] We are, therefore, our own masters. This stream flowed from Nietzsche through Darwin, Freud, and others to its current place, firmly fixed in our contemporary world. A happy life is one of maximizing pleasure (especially sexual pleasure), and anyone who suggests the contrary is clearly in the wrong.

Why should I even grow up, then? In a way, the phenomenon of delayed adolescence—evident across the Western World—illustrates our aimlessness and fixation on living in a cocoon of safety over the adventure of autonomy and risk-taking. "Adulting" is now a pejorative term, something to be delayed as long as possible, for therein lies the death of self-centeredness. The rise of endless Hollywood remakes and reboots perhaps speaks to our obsession with nostalgia and the need to remain in youthful adolescence as long as possible. "Today's child is growing up absurd," says McLuhan, "because he lives in two worlds, and neither of them inclines him to grow up."[52]

But to return to the sense of complete control the modern man and woman ought to command over their lives, consider this chillingly and hubris-filled wording from the 1993 Supreme Court case *Planned Parenthood v. Casey*, a legal ruling that the states were prohibited from banning most abortions: "At the heart of liberty is the right to define one's own concept of existence, of meaning, of the universe, and of the mystery of human life. Beliefs about these matters could not define the attributes of personhood were they formed under compulsion of the State."[53]

[51] Carl R. Trueman, *Strange New World: How Thinkers and Activists Redefined Identity and Sparked the Sexual Revolution* (Wheaton, IL: Crossway, 2022), 62.

[52] Marshall McLuhan, Quentin Fiore, and Jerome Agel, *The Medium Is the Message* (Berkley, CA: Gingko Press, 1996), 18.

[53] Planned Parenthood of Southeastern Pa. v. Casey, 505 U.S. 833 (1992), https://www.law.cornell.edu/supct/html/91-744.ZO.html.

The American courts of the 1700s could never produce such a ruling, but a generation that has drunk of postmodernism and assumed its posture toward the point and purpose of existence certainly can—and has. (One can't help asking, why should we convict the killer of a pregnant woman of "double homicide," when a mother can terminate her pregnancy for any reason she likes, or for no reason at all?)

Read again the fascinating wording of that excerpt from the legal brief: *At the heart of liberty is the right to define one's own concept of existence.* Nothing could be more descriptive of the postmodern, self-creating identity as this. Even my maleness or femaleness is now subject to change.

Near the end of her massive work *The Second Sex*, feminist author Simone de Beauvoir asserted that "nothing is natural."[54] The premise behind the statement is that we create our own reality. We even determine what it means to be a woman or a man. It was this line of thinking that would inspire the next wave of feminist thinkers and, ironically, mutate into the goal of a truly androgynous society. Writers like Judith Butler sought to dismantle even the categories of male and female. Indeed, in a few short decades, "Women's Studies" has morphed into "Gender Studies," as even the concept of what a woman is has become absolutely liquid and infinitely malleable. "What is a woman?" was once—up until a few years ago—considered a useless question, too obvious even to be rhetorical. Now it's both a landmine and a litmus test.

As noted in the previous chapter, technological advances certainly give us the illusion that we are "freer." On the anonymous

[54] Simone de Beauvoir, *The Second Sex*, trans. Constance Borde and Sheila Malovany-Chevallier (New York: Vintage, 2011), 761.

Internet, I can shape every facet of myself, presenting only the edited avatar I desire to be. Humanity has always sought a degree of escapism, which is healthy to a degree. The imagination can truly take flight, for instance, in the playful avenues of the imagination, whether manifested in child's play, literature, film, or video games. But when the desire to escape reality wholesale takes over, and when a person becomes more and more dissatisfied with his or her body, the temptation to escape becomes terrifyingly real.

For many who have been seduced by the allure of "changing" their biological sex, the intense discomfort with their body can finally find relief in the promises offered by transgender ideology.

Underneath all of this is the dark Marxist undercurrent of desired societal change built upon the Nietzschean "will to power" over our sex itself. "The transgender movement is inherently political," asserts author and activist Christopher Rufo:

> Its reconstruction of personal identity is meant to advance a collective political reconstruction or transformation. Some trans activists even view their movement as the future of Marxism. In a collection of essays titled *Transgender Marxism*, activist writer Rosa Lee argues that trans people can serve as the new vanguard of the proletariat, promising to abolish heteronormativity in the same way that orthodox Marxism promised to abolish capitalism.[55]

Of course, if there's an action, there's always a reaction.

[55] Christopher F. Rufo, "Inside the Transgender Empire," *Imprimis*, September 2023, 2.

A Counterrevolution of Common Sense

Consider this ministerial phrase that I so love and often employ: "It makes sense." When we look at the state of men and how men are treated in the world today, it's no wonder that the postmodern landscape has left males utterly confused as to what their role is and how to offer their masculine gifts for the service of others.

Having taught at an all-boys school, this issue is close to my heart, as I saw young men grappling with all the normal questions of masculinity in a world devoid of a script for what being a man means, sometimes doubting whether their masculinity was even wanted. Even asking a girl out on a date could be seen as engaging in "unwanted behavior" or being a "creeper," so of course the safer option for these young men was to retreat inward to either the sanctuary of the self or the illusory harem of pornography. And I couldn't blame them: their fear of being "cancelled" over simply asking a girl on a date was not entirely unjustified.

The #MeToo movement, which began from Hollywood actresses being mistreated by (primarily but not exclusively) men and trickled out into the greater culture, gave voice to victims in an area that needed attention, and many felt the freedom to speak and unburden themselves of harmful, unwanted sexual experiences. The subsequent #BelieveAllWomen trend continued this train of thought that sought to empower victims of abusive situations. And, to be sure, it's good that these women (and not a few men) came forward to expose the men who victimized them and to shed light on Hollywood's culture of complicity. Yet the #MeToo movement quickly became weaponized and went beyond its initial realm. Women with malicious intent could now slander any man and walk away the victor—from celebrities to college students to wives in divorce courts.

And now we're seeing the reaction to the reaction. Against the attempted flattening of male and female (with men competing in women's sports and the multiplication of gender identities), we see the rise of the über-male, the "red-pilled" Alpha of the Internet who leans back to a hyper-masculine physique. Or the feminine answer of fitting into the role of the docile "trad wife," with mandatory prairie aesthetic. Neither response is necessarily wrong—there are plenty who feel comfortable with and called to such aesthetics—but the problem is when we try to create an arbitrary one-size-fits-all caricature of masculinity and femininity.

Is there perhaps a third option, by which we can ground ourselves in the objective duality of man and woman while also opening a nuanced, wide spectrum for how masculinity and femininity are lived by the individual person?

Chapter 11

Tribalism as Telos

Here's a quick recap of what we've covered so far: With the loss of an objective standard of God and His law, we have no subsequent basis for morality and truth, goodness and beauty. Anything ugly or incongruent can be considered art. There is no greater good of human behavior to consider, only what brings the most power.

Under the spell of omnipresent technology that gives us the illusion of control of our own nature, we are left believing that we can change even our biology, including the very nature of male and female.

All of the aforementioned elements that we are grappling with in this era of postmodernity have led us to this point of total psychosocial disorientation.

Identity: Who am I? Where do I fit in and belong? Who is with me?

And deriving from that, what is my telos—my mission, my purpose?

Whose Tribe Are You On?

The human species is a fundamentally *religious* species. The Latin root of the word *religion, religare*, means "to bind together." To the extent that we are communal creatures, we all find ties that bind us together. Even if it's not "organized religion," we all bind ourselves to one another in various forms of group identity: Democrat, Republican, vegan, carnivore, CrossFitter, cosplayer, and so on. There's no escaping the need to form communities.

This is what Aristotle meant when he said that man is a "political animal." He wasn't saying that we love stump speeches and yard signs. He was referring to the Greek word *polis*, which is the root of politics. The polis is the city, the homeland, the community. We need each other. We can't flourish in isolation.[56] As God the Father put it, "It is not good that the man should be alone" (Gen. 2:18, NRSVCE).

What is new about our era is the constellation of the elements explored in our previous chapters: the abstraction of truth and meaning; the atomizing and isolating effects of technology and social media; the victimhood/revolutionary mentality creeping into every facet of life; and even the loss of a steady grounding in what it means to be male and female. The anonymous and disembodied nature of the Internet (both as a tool and a medium of communication) further leads to the fragmentation of our nature. I can say things behind the comfort of a screenname that I would never say to my neighbor's face.

As the COVID pandemic of 2020–2021 stretched on, the Make America Great Again hat and the medical facemask alike became political symbols (now we're using "politics" in the ordinary, everyday sense). They were tribal identifiers. They marked one out

[56] Hermits may seem like the exception that proves the rule. Yet, technically, the Christian tradition holds that a man or woman may only become a hermit for the sake of growing in love for his or her fellow man. The goal is to attain a deeper, purer fellowship with all mankind through prayer and fasting. Becoming a hermit is a deeply "political" act in the Aristotelian sense!

as being "of the Right" or "of the Left." And we're being trained more and more to hate one another. It used to be a rosary that hung from the rearview mirrors of every other car that passed by. Now you're just as likely to see a mask or a dreamcatcher dangling from the mirror, a fitting reflection of where someone's ultimate trust lies.

Without any anchoring in an external, unchanging Truth that unites a populace, the descent into barbarism is almost guaranteed. For us, it has begun online with the anonymity of the "cancel-culture" mob that is out for blood, in many ways no different than the ancient Romans in the Colosseum.

No wonder there is a rise in indifference and cruelty. We shrug our shoulders at the latest mugging or shooting spree. "That same force which ignores human dignity," wrote Hilaire Belloc, "also ignores human suffering."[57] We are a generation obsessed with "social justice" and yet so quick to belittle, scapegoat, and ostracize those who think differently from what the acceptable narrative of pop culture is at the time.

Once a society loses its foundation of belief in the individual as made in the *imago Dei* and replaces this with group identity or statist presumptions, then Hell on earth is right around the corner. Be it scapegoating calls for "cancellations" of a person, state-sanctioned gulags, or ethnic cleansing, the deeper impulse is fundamentally the same. "With no objective standard by which to mediate their different perspectives and feelings, and with no appeal to reason possible," writes Stephen Hicks, "group balkanization and conflict must necessarily result." [58]

[57] Hilaire Belloc, *The Great Heresies* (Rockford, IL: TAN Books, 1991), 262.

[58] Stephen R. C. Hicks, *Explaining Postmodernism: Skepticism and Socialism from Rousseau to Foucault*, exp. ed. (Roscoe, IL: Ockham's Razor Publishing, 2011), 82.

What we *are* in the truest sense is the image and likeness of God. This is our identity. To define ourselves by group memberships—especially those of a victim group, whether real or perceived—is to root our identities in something less than fundamental. It doesn't speak to our innermost self. And for that reason, it will never satisfy our desire for authenticity and self-knowledge. We are *more* than our skin color, our nationality, our economic class, our sexual desires, our political views, our hobbies, or any other superficial attribute.

Greater minds than my own have conjectured that at the heart of the postmodern predicament is the ultimate rejection of authority. The postmodern individual (i.e., everyone alive today) is one who is in charge of his or her own destiny, who is beholden to no one else, and who is in the supreme creative chair of his or her own self-expression and destiny in life.

It all sounds so alluring. And so it was for Adam and Eve in the Garden when tempted by the Serpent. "You shall be as gods," Satan whispers in their ears (Gen. 3:5, DRA). The devil doesn't lie outright, but he does twist—or "deconstruct"—the words of God's message.

At the heart of the postmodern predicament is the rejection of not just authority but *fatherhood* in particular. It's no wonder that men have acutely felt the fallout of having their masculinity belittled, their capacity for servant leadership stripped, and the grand project of fatherhood reviled. We need men of great soul now more than ever, but many have been scared into hiding.

Underneath it all, it's ultimately God's fatherhood that is attacked, and this is the biggest void we seek to fill. We've been taught that, God being dead and all, we've been abandoned by the cosmos. And we're supposed to be okay with that. But deep in the recess of the human heart, we rebel—and we rebel against our own rebellion. *This is not enough*, we feel. We want more. We feel as if we were made for more. Like impulsive toddlers, we delight in self-creation but also torment ourselves by it, desperately awaiting the arrival of a parent to lead us to sanity.

As much as we rebel against the Father, we desperately need Him.

Part 3

The Recovery

Chapter 12

"Seed Packets"

HALFWAY THROUGH MY undergraduate studies, long before I ever dreamed that I would be a teacher, I went on a study abroad trip to Ireland. It was a two-week, two-credit course in Irish folk music that had absolutely *nothing* to do with my major; I just wanted to go to Ireland.

As an American, I stuck out like a sore thumb, drinking my daily Guinness in the "heat" of the summer. But the locals were happy to accommodate me. I stayed an additional two weeks on my own to travel, surf (in a *very* thick wetsuit), and climb Croagh Padraic, the mountain St. Patrick himself traversed to offer penance in the fifth century.

One of my favorite memories of that trip was the spontaneous stops on the country roads to explore the ruins of old stone chapels and unknown buildings being reclaimed by the emerald hills. These structures, and the people who inhabited and used them, are largely a mystery to us today; many who used them are lost to history forever, known only to the mind of God. One particular hollowed-out church my classmates and I examined had Latin inscriptions in its stonework, and the Celtic crosses that littered its adjacent field left us quiet and pensive. The sacred space commanded our reverence thousands of years after it fell into disuse.

These decayed shells of churches long gone can be haunting and sobering images. On the one hand, the ruins of the past are a *memento-mori* message: a reminder of our own mortality. They keep a measure of humility in this life, for the bells of death will always toll for thee and no one gets out of this life alive.

These ruins can also be unsettling images that seem to foreshadow the future of our own Church: emptied buildings long abandoned by believers, a faith that has died and should be left to the shelves of history. Even for people of a more humanistic or secular way of being in the world, this brave new postmodern landscape can be unnerving and disorienting. We usually don't know what we have until it's gone.

The metaphor of a beautiful bouquet of flowers cut off from the ground and sitting in a vase has been used to describe our modern situation. We can ride on the fumes of our Judeo-Christian sense of morality, natural rights, the rule of law, and the dignity of the human person—at least for a while. Cut off from the roots that anchor us in God and virtue, however, it's no surprise that we're withering. One can feel it in certain cultures almost palpably, that a sense of purpose has been lost. "While nihilism may be understandable in some individuals," writes journalist Douglas Murry (an atheist), "as a societal creed it is fatal."[59]

"Cut flowers die," said noted author, human-rights activist and Christian convert Ayaan Hirsi Ali in a panel conversation with thought leaders Jordan Peterson, John Anderson, and Os Guinness. That is true, cut flowers do die. But what we have in terms of Western civilization is a lot of "seed packets." It's so tempting to focus on the negative and the obstacles ahead of us as

[59] Douglas Murray, *The Strange Death of Europe: Immigration, Identity, Islam* (London, Bloomsbury Continuum, 2018), 266

we try to piece back together what has been torn apart. But Ali turns our attention toward what we do have instead. "We have the remnants, the symbols of Western heritage, and all we have to do is go and seed them, grow them, nurture them, water them, and when they are attacked, fight for them."[60]

Think back to the introduction of this book and the comment my student made: "Mr. Angel, it's like we're back at the *beginning* of philosophy again. We don't even know what is true anymore." Indeed, but we have the seed packets of the great minds who have come before us. We have the remnants of Socrates and Augustine. We've been given contemporary examples such as St. John Paul II and Edith Stein.

In his preface to the prescient work *From Christendom to Apostolic Mission*, Msgr. James Shea names the modern problem that many leaders in the Church either have yet to face or are reluctant to admit: we are not in an age of comfortable Christendom anymore. Rather, we are living in a secularized and antagonistic culture that calls for an apostolic offensive. He begins by citing the words of Archbishop Fulton Sheen in 1974 (which could be an echo of the observation of Nietzsche): "We are at the end of Christendom. Not of Christianity, not of the Church, but of Christendom.... That is ending, we've seen it die." But unlike Nietzsche's doom-filled celebration, Sheen called forth courage and joy: "These are great and wonderful days in which to be alive.... It is not a gloomy picture—it is a picture of the Church in the midst of increasing opposition from the world."[61]

[60] "Panel: What is the West?" Alliance for Responsible Citizenship, video, 49:29, October 30, 2023, https://www.youtube.com/watch?v=wtZq-zF1QG4.

[61] Quoted in Monsignor James P. Shea, preface to *From Christendom to Apostolic Mission*, ii.

The waters ahead will not be smooth sailing, but calm seas never made strong sailors. And Christ promised that He would be with us until the end of this age. At the close of *Fides et Ratio*, St. John Paul II called for leaders to recover the search for human good, to be confident that truth can be known, and to stand anew upon the ground of *being*. "We face a great challenge at the end of this millennium to move from *phenomenon* to *foundation*.... We cannot stop short at experience alone."[62] We can have one foot in our subjective experience (our stories) while the other foot is anchored in the objective truth outside ourselves, Truth that we believe has encountered us in the person of Jesus Christ.

The remaining chapters are by no means the "silver bullet" for regaining a sense of sanity today, but I do hope and pray that out of the depths of this abyss we might start to rebuild, and I offer a roadmap in the pages ahead.

62 Pope John Paul II, *Fides et Ratio*, no. 83.

Chapter 13

Stories and Truth

"But they have conquered him by the blood of the Lamb and by the word of their testimony, for they did not cling to life even in the face of death."—Revelation 12:11

As we've seen throughout this text, the postmodern shift places a dramatic emphasis on "storytelling," as subjective narratives now hold proportionately greater weight than appeals to objective standards, natural law, or historical documentation. We don't conform ourselves to existence; rather, existence is now expected to bend to my story ("my truth"). A person's "lived experience" trumps any notion of conforming one's behavior to an external code.

Since we as human beings tend to swing from one extreme to another, we can see where this emphasis on pure storytelling versus objective facts is taken too far. The effort to fight injustice and share the untold stories of the nation's marginalized populations has mutated into an Orwellian effort to rewrite history. Statues have been torn down, schools rebranded, and holidays abolished or renamed to be more in keeping with modern, progressive sensibilities. With the tools of new technology, it is easier than ever to deceptively edit videos, change articles, or destroy past periodicals, so that the only history we pass on is the one our technocrats have approved for us to know. "They should have known better" is one of the stones we throw today. "I would have spoken out. I would have been different."

Now, in some instances, it is beneficial to reassess the whitewashed stories we've been told of national heroes and acknowledge disreputable behavior where it has occurred. There is indeed a great benefit to hearing the untold stories of history and reckoning in gray instead of bifurcating history into simplistic black and white. All these events must be evaluated without haste, which I know is easier said than done in our culture today.

History and humanity are complex. We are all a mixture of the light and the dark, and the best of men and women throughout history were still fallen and flawed. Anyone trying to live up to the standards of the current hour will be doomed by those who arrive next week. As Venerable Fulton Sheen wrote, "The Church knows too that to marry the present age and its spirit is to become a widow in the next."[63]

Can there be room for mercy? Is there space for nuance and forgiveness? Are we willing to remove the logs in our own eyes before pointing out the splinters in everyone else's?

✠ ✠ ✠

One positive in this shift is that we *love* stories and stories can indeed convey deep truths. Kids love rewatching their favorite movies over and over again. We adults have our stories we revisit time and again. (The actor Christopher Lee read the *Lord of the Rings* trilogy every year—even before he played Saruman in the movies!) Jesus himself used parables and stories, knowing that their lessons cut deeper into hearts than declarations of moral precepts would. Stories, especially personal testimonies, can further shed light on what the traditional historical record might have occluded.

[63] Fulton J. Sheen, *Old Errors and New Labels* (New York: Society of St. Paul, 2007), 50.

The nuanced response looks for what *good* there might be in this new turn toward the subjective while keeping a foot anchored in the objective. "You experienced *this* situation," we might say to a person who suffered some form of abuse, injustice, or neglect, "and are right to feel that way." Is there more to the picture, though?

One way to anchor this turn toward the subjective is to offer the sometimes challenging counter question: "But is that true? Is there more to it?"

There's also the simple task of listening to one another, resisting the temptation to argue with or preach at the other person. I remember one painful moment in my formation when this was hammered home. I was standing in the community room of a drug and alcohol rehab center in Miami. This was during my first year of seminary formation and the work was extremely humbling. I saw well-established professionals brought to rock bottom by substance abuse. There was no teaching or quote from the *Summa Theologica* that could make it all right. These men and women desperately needed to be seen, heard, and validated as they were seeking to get their lives back on track.

I'll never forget the middle-aged woman who walked up to me one day and asked bluntly, "You work for God?"

"I'm in formation to be a Catholic priest, ma'am," I told her.

"Okay then, preacher. Tell me why God would take the lives of both of my sons in an ATV accident four years ago?"

Now I was surprised. Surprised and speechless.

After maybe ten seconds that felt like ten hours, this woman, whose eyes burned with intense anger and hurt, turned and left me, stunned and fumbling over my words, and I never saw her again.

It's often the case that when people come to you to share their problems, they aren't really looking for advice so much as to be heard. People want their pain to be understood and their story to matter. There is certainly time to give instruction and to teach. But people will never care to listen until they first sense that we care about them.

The sharing of testimonies has long been a part of the Christian Faith. "Always be prepared to make a defense to any one who calls you to account for the hope that is in you," St. Peter instructed almost two thousand years ago, "yet do it with gentleness and reverence" (1 Pet. 3:15, RSVCE). Truth should never be wielded as a hammer, but proposed and offered, respecting the free will of the person before us.

Kat Von D, a well-known entrepreneur and celebrity tattoo artist, took many by surprise (myself included) when she announced her conversion to Christianity in 2023. Though she had been raised in a Christian household, she largely rejected the faith and poured her energy into tattoo artistry in her late teens. She became an alcoholic in her twenties while being showcased on the TV shows *Miami Ink* and *LA Ink*. As she was achieving sobriety, she found solace in New Age spiritualisms such as tarot cards and occult readings. "I was a seeker, not pursuing any belief system, I was just sad.... It was always these short-lived band-aids on a sinking ship."[64]

But she began watching sermons and reading the Bible as an adult during the upheaval of the 2020 pandemic, which led to a great deal of reevaluating her life and perspectives. She threw away her New Age books and eventually posted a video of her Baptism online that gained millions of views. "I'm on fire for Jesus.... I want to worship, I don't want to go to a concert, I want to learn about the Bible, not feel-good stories," she

64 "Kat Von D on Becoming a Christian," Allie Beth Stuckey, video, 00:24:24, November 6, 2023, https://www.youtube.com/watch?v=ZLfIjbOXgY0.

affirmed, noting that she's finally found the depth and meaning of life she'd been seeking.[65]

No one is ever "too far gone" from the love and mercy of God.

It is not the Church's job to be popular. Jesus' call to purify our hearts, uphold the dignity of every human person, from womb to tomb, and submit in humble trust before a Father we can trust is absolutely countercultural.

To present yourself as a disciple of Christ (or even to assert a simple belief in a standard of natural law) is today, naturally, to invite rejection, mockery, scapegoating, and even martyrdom. The wisdom of God will of course appear backward, foolish, absurd, and "phobic" in the eyes of the world (see 1 Corinthians 1:18–25).

A major portion of the work ahead is to appeal to this innate call for reintegration of the human person, to listen empathetically to the stories and suffering before us, and to help others regain a sense of anchoring in objective truth and a purposeful life. Once we have listened and gained the trust of another, there is a point at which we must share the truth.

Alexander Solzhenitsyn, the Nobel laureate and anti-Communist dissident, wrote a book called *The Gulag Archipelago*, which exposed the totalitarianism of the Soviet Union. He once believed in the promises of the Communist revolution, but after his persecution by the state and years in the gulag prison system, he felt compelled to expose its facilities. Before he was exiled from Moscow, he published a speech entitled "Live Not by Lies!" in which he implored ordinary men and women never to go along with falsehoods out of fear. We can live in the dignity of the truth, even if the world has lost its mind.

[65] Ibid. 00:36:36; 00:44:26

To reclassify *disorder as order* forgoes the possibility of recovery, Abigail Favale notes, for the "cure for this disease [of rejecting the body] cannot be its cause. The balm for dis-integration cannot be found in further entropy."[66] Fragmentation can never lead to wholeness. And sharing or shouting lies about the body or the human condition does not make them true. Live not by lies!

One of my favorite books to gift to my former students at their graduation was Viktor Frankl's *Man's Search for Meaning*. Frankl, an Austrian psychiatrist who survived the Nazi death camps, resumed his practice upon his liberation and became convicted of the power of a life lived, not for mere pleasure or "self-actualization," but in the pursuit of meaning and service. "Logotherapy," Frankl wrote, "focuses on the meaning of human existence … This striving to find a meaning in one's life is the primary motivational force in man."[67]

Frankl knew that, in the worst of all situations and in the darkest of times, those who clung to hope and a higher purpose could endure any evil. "The existential vacuum which is the mass neurosis of the present time can be described as a private and personal form of nihilism."[68] People are starving for the truth. Comfort and entertainment can only numb us for so long. Eventually, the big questions start to catch up and we need to be brave enough to share the truth.

When a therapeutic and medical culture of self-harm and mutilation is rebranded as "self-care," we have to be courageous enough to say "No." When our young people are so desperately confused, drowning in nihilism and entertainment, and in despair

66 Favale, *Genesis of Gender*, 196, 232.

67 Viktor E. Frankl, *Man's Search for Meaning* (Boston: Beacon Press, 2006), 98–99.

68 Ibid., 129.

of the future, we can extend a hand and let them know that they are not alone, that life is worth living, and that they can find meaning in a life given away for others.

Our children and grandchildren depend on it.

Chapter 14

Gift and Beauty

While "the culture of meh," as I described in an earlier chapter, is strong indeed among our generation, I believe that underneath that jadedness and cynicism lies a desire to stumble upon something—anything—that can jar awake the human heart that aches for joy.

The 1999 Academy Award best picture *American Beauty* was a dark comedy/drama that demonstrates the meltdown of a suburban father named Lester Burnham and his family. At first glance, it appears profoundly postmodern in its nihilism and materialistic outlook. The characters, as in so much of contemporary film, are all profoundly miserable, but they are all searching for some inkling of happiness in life.

The film ends with a monologue by Lester, which we hear as a montage of all the people interwoven in his life passes by the screen. "It's hard to stay mad," he says, "when there's so much beauty in the world. Sometimes I feel like I'm seeing it all at once, and it's too much. My heart fills up like a balloon that's about to burst. And then I remember to relax, and stop trying to hold on to it, and then it flows through me like rain, and I can't feel anything but gratitude for every single moment of my stupid little life."[69] The montage features a now-iconic shot of a plastic grocery bag floating in the wind. It's a symbol of how even such a cheap, banal, utilitarian, and quintessentially *modern* item can seize our attention, awaken our sense of wonder, and be transformed into a thing of beauty. The wind that plays through the bag is a gift. The moment of interplay between air and plastic is a gift. And Lester's response—which is the proper response—is gratitude.

Gratitude and gift. Gratitude is a powerful antidote to a self-centered life, and seeing the whole of human life—the breath in our lungs, the human interactions all around us, even sorrow and death—as a gift reframes the whole of existence. We reawaken to beauty and, if we follow the thread, the author and source of beauty who is God. Beauty can be like a magnet that stirs and stops us in our tracks, shaking us awake. It arrests us and demands our attention. There's a reason people seek out sunsets and mountain peaks, the *Mona Lisa* and the Cathedral of Notre Dame.

Beauty, art, music, architecture, and stories all can reveal the truth of who we are as human beings and redirect us to this way of being and living fully alive. There's a beautiful movement to restore Church architecture happening across the United States. From California to Connecticut, from Tennessee to Texas, church buildings are being constructed (or refurbished) to reclaim the Catholic Church's Gothic, Romanesque, and Neoclassical heritage.

Roger Scruton wrote that beauty, whether in film, music, architecture, or the human person, "makes a claim on us: it is a call to renounce our narcissism and look with reverence on the world."[70] A life without beauty makes us inhuman. We're not *meant* to work in

[69] *American Beauty*, directed by Sam Mendes (Dreamworks Pictures, 1999).

[70] Roger Scruton, *Beauty: A Very Short Introduction* (New York: Oxford University Press, 2011), 145.

windowless, concrete bunkers and cubicles under fluorescent light. These environments inherently suck the life out of us.

We all worship something. *Worship* means "to give your highest worth to," and whether that's Hollywood, the NFL, the environment, or health and fitness, we all give our highest worth to something. If God is not at the top of that hierarchy, then we will quickly make secondary and tertiary things into idols of worship.

"Nature abhors a vacuum," the saying goes. Whenever we remove something, another object will inevitably take its place. If we've cut off the source of common telos and purpose across Western civilization, if all talk of God and a right ordering of life vanishes, *something* must take its place.

For instance, I've noticed over the last several years an uptick of interest in the philosophy of Stoicism, especially among young men. This ancient approach to dealing with the cold realities of life offers at least some framework for living and coping with one's natural emotions in the world. In the absence of any existing moral framework, Stoicism is meeting an important need for the direction of people's energies.

Psychedelics are also enjoying something of a renaissance, and approval of their use is more widespread than ever. Ayahuasca and ayahuasca-based retreats offer a chance for people to take "healing" trips on these hallucinogens in a safe, controlled environment. New Age practices abound and hold an increasing grip on the younger generations, with Gen Z now seeking to "manifest" their desires to a (supposedly) caring universe that runs on karma.

To the extent we don't know why we're here and what we're made for, we will continue to flounder as a species and grasp at all the aforementioned remedies. We might be able to numb or distract ourselves moment-to-moment in order to cope with life's grief and high questions, but we're made for more than coping mechanisms and bad trips, and the human heart knows this.

"Our ability to *tell the truth* about our own condition, in measured words and touching melodies, offers a kind of redemption from it," Roger Scruton writes. For instance, "T. S. Eliot's *The Waste Land* describes the modern city as a soulless desert: but it does so with images and allusions that affirm what the city denies. Our very ability to make this judgement is the final disproof of it. If we can grasp the emptiness of modern life, this is because art points to *another way of being*."[71]

"Denying nature denies the portals of one's own flesh, leaving one's understanding without a hold on reality," wrote Thomas Aquinas.[72] Those words are an apt diagnosis of our modern malady.

Carl Trueman affirms the need of recognizing the beauty of our creation as male and female and honors the Catholic tradition in holding fast to the teachings on our embodied sex:

> The church also needs to recover natural law and a theology of the body. Roman Catholics have a long tradition with regard to the former and, in the person of Pope John Paul II, a brilliant teacher of the latter....
>
> The world in which we live is not simply morally indifferent "stuff" but possess in itself a moral structure. Our bodies in particular have a profound significance....

71 Scruton, *Beauty*, 139.

72 Thomas Aquinas, *Exposition of Aristotle's Treatise on the Heavens*, trans. Fabian R. Larcher and Pierre H. Conway (Columbus, OH: College of St. Mary on the Springs, 1964), bk. 1, lecture 9, no. 97.

> Biblical teaching is not an arbitrary imposition on nature but instead correlates with it. In other words, [natural law] assists us in showing that God's commands make sense, given the way the world actually is.[73]

So what is natural law? As the *Catechism of the Catholic Church* teaches,

> The natural law, present in the heart of each man and established by reason, is universal in its precepts and its authority extends to all men....
>
> The natural law is immutable and permanent throughout the variations of history; it subsists under the flux of ideas and customs and supports their progress.... Even when it is rejected in its very principles, it cannot be destroyed or removed from the heart of man. It always rises again in the life of individuals and societies.[74]

No matter what means might be used to obfuscate the reality of male and female, or the violence that might be done to mutilate or sterilize our young people, human nature cannot be changed. Our very bones—and every cell of our bodies—speak to our creation in maleness and femaleness. And while different, male and female are complementary and equal in dignity.

What's also needed is a deeper reverence for the true range possible within male and female. As we examined in an earlier

[73] Trueman, *Strange New World*, 182–185.

[74] *Catechism of the Catholic Church*, nos. 1956, 1958.

chapter, human cultures have always fluctuated between flattening the difference between the sexes and creating rigid categories (career, fashion, hobbies) of what constitutes a "true" man or woman. In the flattening of what constitutes a man or woman, of course the reactionary swing will be to jump to the extremes.

"We need to avoid the extremes of forced androgyny on the one hand, and inflexible stereotypes on the other," writes scholar Ryan T. Anderson. "We need to allow boys and girls to express their sex-based differences and their individuality."[75] A framework based on sexual complementarity is one that reverences an equal-in-dignity but different-in-gifts approach to men and women, avoiding the extremes that we see on display all around us.[76]

Personalism

I think one of the most concrete ways forward is the philosophical movement of *personalism*, a way of approaching both the outer objective world as "really real" as well as holding in tension the valid, subjective, interior experience unique to each human person. In Catholicism, it's the beauty of the *both/and*, not either/or (body and soul, male and female, Heaven and Earth, Christ's humanity and divinity).

In one of his first books, *Love and Responsibility*, St. John Paul built upon the moral imperative that the philosopher Immanuel Kant tried to establish in the eighteenth century. Kant believed that people should be treated as their own ends and not as objects

75 Ryan T. Anderson, *When Harry Became Sally: Responding to the Transgender Moment* (New York: Encounter Books, 2018), 156.

76 The writings of Sr. Prudence Allen, R.S.M, contain tremendous insights into how we have moved from sex polarity to reverse sex polarity to fractional complementarity to the concept of integral sexual complementarity as affirmed by St. John Paul II.

or means to an end; John Paul affirmed that "the personalist norm says that the person is a good toward which the only proper and adequate attitude is love."[77]

To orient ourselves as such means that the question is never "How far is too far?" Rather, we should only ask ourselves how we can more perfectly reverence and honor this person before us. It's the application of Christ's command "Whatever you wish that men would do to you, do so to them" (Matt. 7:12, RSVCE), and it invites us to go beyond mere moral commands to pierce our hearts so that we can look upon every man and women as a unique, unrepeatable human being.

To have such a personalistic posture toward every person we encounter is thus the challenge, be it to our employer or employee, our colleague or cashier, our spouse or distant relative or stranger across the globe. Whether a person is healthy or crippled, in utero or standing on an Olympic podium, it makes no difference because he or she is a person due all dignity as a child of God. This way of life reverences the interior subject of the person without falling into a subjectivism that reduces reality to *my* experiences and feelings.

The behavior codes on college campuses have been centered around the concept of "consent," which although helpful, doesn't go far enough when it comes to true education in a respect for the dignity of each human person who ought not be treated as an object of use. It degrades both men and women wholesale, even if it is behavior I have "consented" to. "I am in my body, not as a 'ghost in the machine,' but as an incarnate self," wrote Scruton, arguing for a regrounding in a person-oriented take on moral behavior: "My body is identical with me: subject and object are

[77] Karol Wojtyla (Pope John Paul II), *Love and Responsibility*, trans. H.T. Willetts (San Francisco: Ignatius Press, 1981), 41.

merely two aspects of a single thing.... Sexual virtue does not forbid desire: it simply ensures the status of desire as an interpersonal feeling."[78]

A personalistic philosophy thus is a bulwark against the destructive philosophies of our day. An attitude of utilitarianism, for instance, looks at people only for their *utility*—they are worthy of importance only if they are "useful" or capable of giving pleasure; if they're not contributing, they should be discarded. Or those who believe in the debunked ideas of Thomas Malthus (1766–1834), who taught that populations must be reduced in order to avoid global catastrophe, in order to justify the thinking that we need *fewer* human beings on the planet for the sake of combatting climate change. (No one seems to want to address *which* human people should be reduced, though. The proponents of population reduction are almost never willing to include themselves in those calculations.)

A personalistic approach always keeps the individual person at the forefront of one's interactions. Revered author and artist Michael O'Brien writes that "the Church is neither collectivist nor individualist. She is personalist," always keeping the dignity of the person at the fore. "Where the Church sees each human being as a person in need of formation and salvation, the collectivist mind sees a social problem in need of rehabilitation."[79]

So much of the Marxist framework and "errors of Russia spread around the world" entail the fight against our God-given design as man and woman, persons imbued with equal dignity despite our complementary differences. Consumed with pride, we

[78] Roger Scruton, *An Intelligent Person's Guide to Philosophy* (New York: Penguin, 1996), 137.

[79] Michael D. O'Brien, *The Family and the New Totalitarianism* (n.p.: Divine Providence Press, 2000), 59–60.

fight tooth and claw to be more than we are, trying to control our environment, mutating viruses, and daring to think that we can "change" our very sex. "The Church knows that collectivist and reductionary approaches to the human person fail, and always produce as much damage as any good they do," O'Brien notes. Only a personalistic approach is rightfully "concerned with the salvation of each human person as an irrepeatable and mysterious epiphany of the mind of God."[80]

Descartes's legacy is one that sees the solitary human person as the only surety in the world, and even then, pits his mind against his bodily reality. But the reality is that I come to know myself as one who is *in relation* to others. "Yet this is phenomenologically inside out," writes professor of philosophy Chad Engelland. "It is the presence of things that is more manifest than self-presence.... My own face is ordinarily hidden from me and my own presence inconspicuous. The faces of others light up, revealing their thoughts. My face is shown to me only though the look of others' responses."[81]

I am revealed in relationship with others. While I can certainly be *with* others in a disembodied way over Internet chat boxes or video calls (and those *can* be good and healthy forms of connection), I am made for more than pixelated relationships. We find ourselves by giving ourselves away—by becoming a gift. This paradox is on full display in the sacrifice of Christ, who offers Himself up for our freedom and invites us to do the same.

[80] Ibid., 121.

[81] Chad Engelland, "With What Must We Begin?" *Communio* 50, no. 3 (Fall 2023): 491.

Chapter 15

Rest: Regaining the Sabbath and Remaining in the Present Moment

"Bloom where you are planted," I see embroidered in every hand towel at the local décor shop. Easier said than done, especially when we are witnessing the rise of one of the most anxiety-ridden generations the world has ever seen.

Twenty-four-hour news and constantly refreshing social media feeds have us feeling responsible, through the burden of knowledge, for those suffering from disasters around the globe. "Too many people know too much about each other," McLuhan observed. (Note that he was speaking before the advent of the Internet!) "Our new environment compels commitment and participation," he continued. "We have become irrevocably involved with, and responsible for each other."[82] On one hand, there is the blessing of awareness of others' plights, prompting us to feel compassion and enabling us to assist when possible. Yet, such knowledge can also lead to paralyzing despair as we confront the magnitude of humankind's need. And for the most

[82] McLuhan, Fiore, and Agel, *Medium Is the Message*, 24.

callous, the pain of another might elicit a mere shrug of indifference: "Not my problem."

In the beginning of this book, I noted that it's tempting to wish we were living in another century or another time, believing that it would be easier back then. If only we were in the thirteenth century, some medieval-lovers might declare. If only we were living in the 1950s before the mess of Vatican II, others could wish. Or take it further: if only we had a different pope or president or pastor...

That statement, "If only," can be helpful as a way of venting one's frustrations. Ultimately, however, it's a form of complaining against God, or punting the ball of personal responsibility down the field. "I *would* do my part to make a change in the world, *if only...*"

For the Christian, a fundamental way to avoid falling into either the trap of despair or the self-important savior complex is to recognize where you are in the present moment and simply help those in your five-mile radius. If you can't feed everyone, feed just *one* person. The Catholic social teaching principle of subsidiarity teaches us that we should put our work toward the local changes that we can address rather than dwelling on problems that are too large or too far away for us to redress effectively. Do what you can, with what you have, in your home territory, before you worry about changing the world.

You also can't give what you don't have. So many of us struggle with workaholism or the need to control our surroundings. As disciples of Christ, we are called to love our weakness, for in it Christ is made strong. Practically speaking, this means surrendering control and allowing God to be the one in charge. We can do this by switching out of the relentless "doing" mode and re-embracing being, and two of the primary ways to do this are simply regaining a sense of the Sabbath and learning to abandon ourselves to the present moment.

In the Old Testament, one of Jeremiah's great struggles was to help the people of Israel remember the promises of God and turn their attention continually back to right worship. The Sabbath was of particular importance to Jeremiah, for the day of rest was vital to giving the Almighty His just due: "As you love your lives, take care not to carry burdens on the sabbath, to bring them in through the gates of Jerusalem. Bring no burden from your homes on the sabbath. Do no work whatever, but keep holy the sabbath day, as I commanded your ancestors" (Jer. 17:21–22, NABRE).

In Christianity, the Sabbath represents the great triumph of the Resurrection of Christ over the gates of death. We now come together to celebrate weekly the Eucharistic Banquet, the source and summit of our faith. We are called to rest from labors that impede worship and rest, reaffirming that humans are not creatures called to endless work but beings made for union with the Divine. Many people (religious and unreligious) have instituted "tech sabbaths" in their homes: days where all devices are powered off and the family can simply *be* with one another, at rest, in nature, and at play. And every year, more people willingly take whole months off of social media to rest and reset their lives.

The yearly liturgical rhythm of the Catholic Church follows the seasons around the sun and celebrates in the continual retelling of the Christian story: the advent and birth of Jesus, His suffering, death, and Resurrection, and the "ordinary" times interspersed through it all. The Sabbath demands that we slow down and regain a sense of God's time. It's not on our shoulders alone to move the powers and principalities and philosophies we are up against. We must let God be God and allow Him to reground us principally in His divine love *before* we undertake any effective action.

Beyond the Sabbath, awareness of the present moment—the here and now, the time that God has called you into—is one of the best ways to restore some sanity and grounding to your own life, and by extension to the lives of others. The seventeenth-century spiritual writer Br. Lawrence of the Resurrection called it "practicing the presence of God." The eighteenth-century Jesuit luminary Fr. Jean-Pierre de Caussade named it "abandonment to Divine Providence." Taking in the moment that God has given you, right now, reading this page with the breath in your lungs, feet on the floor (or propped up on the couch), is the time given to you, and this is where the God of the universe—who is outside of time and space—is *now.*

It's not easy to stay in the present, but it's so important to regain a sense of our bodily self. The temptation to get lost in anxiety over the future or in beating ourselves up over past mistakes is real, indeed. I had a spiritual director once who knew I was keen on ruminating over times I fell short, and he would remind me, "You know God hates it when you beat up on someone He loves." This priest helped me to laugh, reminding me to take my sins seriously but myself not so much. He taught me the simple prayer of St. Padre Pio: "Lord, I leave the past in Your mercy, the future in Your providential care, and the present moment in Your love."

Even humor is a gift that can be wielded as a wonderful tool to bring levity in our dark and confusing times. The postmodern era is full of navel-gazing and irreverent crudities aimed at pure shock, shock that inevitability outstays its welcome and leads to boredom and cynicism. The death of comedy is one of the saddest fruits of postmodernism, but it also awakens in people the thirst for joy that endless deconstruction can never offer. True whimsical humor can cut like a knife through the ennui to reveal the truth beneath the surface. The best comedians are great psychologists and often prophets of a special sort, reminding us of our foibles and flaws and to not take life so seriously.

"Often we become agitated and disturbed by trying to resolve everything ourselves," writes Fr. Jacques Philippe, "when it would be more efficacious to remain peacefully before the gaze of God.... This doesn't mean we should be lazy or inactive. Trusting God is courageously and powerfully active."[83] Indeed, we often can accomplish so much more (and be more at peace) when we simply have the courage to be still.

There is a natural rhythm of work and rest for the human person that is proper to his or her dignity: labor and leisure, play and sleep, fasting and feasting, sorrow and laughter. To regain our humanity in this cacophonous age means slowing down, logging off, and becoming aware of the present moment God has given us.

[83] Jacques Philippe, *Searching for and Maintaining Peace: A Small Treatise on Peace of Heart*, trans. George and Jannic Driscoll (New York: Alba House, 2002), 6.

Chapter 16

Love One Another

THE EARLIEST CHRISTIANS were misunderstood and persecuted. Refusing to make the obligatory sacrifice to Caesar—the "pinch of incense"—many were scapegoated by society. Many others were sent to their deaths. Yet they went happily, knowing that the love they experienced in Christ was far greater than any earthly prestige, power, or wealth.

The first disciples of Christ were ordinary men and women who cared for one another. They took in the abandoned infants deemed "unworthy" of life and supported widows, orphans, and the destitute. They were in the world, but lived differently than the world.

The road of self-sacrifice, whether public and bloody in a coliseum or hidden away in the domestic setting, is an imitation of Jesus' triumphant Resurrection after death. The blood of the martyrs is the seed of the church, wrote Tertullian, one of the earliest Christian theologians. To see someone go to their death wearing the faith of God on their sleeves is something that can convict the hearts of many and bear spiritual fruit of great capacity. "Unless a grain of wheat falls into the earth and dies, it remains alone," Christ told us, "but if it dies, it bears much fruit" (John 12:24, RSVCE).

Nourished by the Eucharist, the very Body and Blood of Christ Himself, and with the help of the Communion of Saints and our mutual support of one another, we can bring light into the darkness. The mission ahead requires a very real martyrdom in the best sense of the word: *witness*. How that plays out is unique to each of our lives, vocations, strengths, skills, and weaknesses. This will entail stepping out of our comfort zones and embracing the challenge Christ has called us to.

At the heart of being a Christian is a personal encounter with God, and that encounter cannot be manufactured. More than conveying commandments and rules, and even propositions and arguments for the faith, we need to start with a person's experience—to "meet them where they are"—and then redirect to the intellect. "Propositions can thus be said to have a second-order importance.... We should employ theological propositions such as 'sin' and 'grace' in order that others might encounter God in Christ and then join us on the grand journey of understanding the meaning of that encounter for all of life."[84]

Dan Burke, one of the greatest spiritual writers alive today, has a saying: "Love builds a bridge over which truth can pass."

Apologetics are important. "Christ came to take away our sins, not our brains!" a seminary professor of mine used to exclaim. But because the postmodern context has taught us to prioritize stories and the subjective, we must meet people there and then patiently lead them to God's doorstep, always respecting their autonomy. Everything in God's time.

In a joint statement with Ecumenical Patriarch Bartholomew I, Pope Benedict XVI affirmed: "We cannot ignore the increase

[84] Stanley J. Grenz, *A Primer on Postmodernism* (Grand Rapids, MI: William B. Eerdmans, 1996), 171.

of secularization, relativism, even nihilism, especially in the Western world. All this calls for a renewed and powerful application of the Gospel, adapted to the cultures of our time."[85] We see the effects of postmodernity all around us. There is much reason to despair, but it is also a time that calls for new creativity and courage: to embrace the media given to us and use it well, to affirm the goodness inherent in each human person regardless of their "usefulness," and to bravely share the gospel that can provide life-giving water to souls dying of spiritua dehydration.

One of the difficulties today is simply evangelizing. We've been beaten over the head to think that sharing our faith in any capacity is equivalent to some form of "colonization"—insisting that our particular way of life is better than someone else's. In a postmodern-relativistic world, that is a huge "no-no." Many of us are, at some level, fearful of the Internet mob that will gleefully harass and dox us if we dare to preach what we actually believe. "Who am I to impose my worldview on someone else?" we might rationalize in our fearfulness.

In the void of affirming what we know to bring goodness and life to others, a counternarrative will *absolutely* sweep into the void. For instance, Nigerian author and biomedical scientist Obianuju Ekeocha calls out the Western ruling elites for their "neocolonial" attitudes toward the African peoples, writing,

> Western governments and organizations sponsor and host meetings, conferences, and summits to discuss African problems. They spearhead extensive

[85] *Common Declaration of Pope Benedict XVI and the Ecumenical Patriarch Bartholomew I* (November 30, 2006), no. 3, https://www.vatican.va/content/benedict-xvi/en/speeches/2006/november/documents/hf_ben-xvi_spe_20061130_dichiarazione-comune.html.

> contraception programs, HIV-prevention campaigns, youth-empowerment projects, and maternal-health initiatives—all of which are based on the assumption that there are not relevant natural, ethical, or cultural norms for sexual behavior or even fixed biological facts concerning sexual identity. Referring to themselves as experts and champions of human rights, they interfere not only in the domestic affairs and laws of African nations but in their definitions of "man," "woman," "marriage," "child," and "family"—all while claiming to be the disinterested "partners of Africa."[86]

There is no "blank slate," no value-neutral communication of ideas. Whenever we try to do good for someone else, we are necessarily acting from some theory of what *the good* entails. "Bad men need nothing more to compass their ends, than that good men should look on and do nothing," John Stuart Mill rightfully observed in 1867.[87] We are constantly being fed a worldview based on *ideas* (philosophies) that have consequences, even if that worldview is a relativistic one: "There is no *right* way to live."

A worldview is always being imposed. Real lives are at stake if we sit back and do nothing.

The situation can be summed up by a passage that deserves to be quoted at length. It is from the introduction to *Gaudium et Spes*,

[86] Obianuju Ekeocha, *Target Africa: Ideological Neocolonialism in the Twenty-First Century* (San Francisco: Ignatius Press, 2019), 138.

[87] *Inaugural Address at St. Andrew's*, 1867, quoted in "John Stuart Mill, 1806–1873," *Oxford Essential Quotations*, 5th ed., ed. Susan Ratcliffe, online at Oxford Reference, 2017, https://www.oxfordreference.com/display/10.1093/acref/9780191843730.001.0001/q-oro-ed5-00007298.

a document of the Second Vatican Council that a young Karol Wojtyla (the future John Paul II) had a direct hand in shaping.

> Many think that they can find peace in the different philosophies that are proposed.
>
> Some look for complete and genuine liberation for man from man's efforts alone. They are convinced that the coming kingdom of man on earth will satisfy all the desires of his heart.
>
> There are those who despair of finding any meaning in life: they commend the boldness of those who deny all significance to human existence in itself, and seek to impose a total meaning on it only from within themselves.
>
> But in the face of the way the world is developing today, there is an ever increasing number of people who are asking the most fundamental questions or are seeing them with a keener awareness: What is man? What is the meaning of pain, of evil, of death, which still persist in spite of such great progress? What is the use of those successes, achieved at such a cost? What can man contribute to society, what can he expect from society? What will come after this life on earth?
>
> The Church believes that Christ died and rose for all, and can give man light and strength through his Spirit to fulfill his highest calling; his is the only name under heaven in which men can be saved.
>
> So too the Church believes that the center and goal of all human history is found in her Lord and Master.

> The Church also affirms that underlying all changes there are many things that do not change; they have their ultimate foundation in Christ, who is the same yesterday, today and for ever.[88]

[88] Second Vatican Council, Pastoral Constitution on the Church in the Modern World *Gaudium et Spes* (December 7, 1965), as rendered in the Office of Readings for Saturday in the First Week of Lent, DivineOffice.org, February 24, 2024, https://divineoffice.org/lent-w01-sat-or/?date=20240224.

Conclusion

"MR. ANGEL, WE'VE been learning all year about these four stages in philosophy. But what's *after* postmodernism?"

I remember this all-too-brief exchange with a senior who had followed along in our philosophy class as best he could, before the COVID-19 pandemic of 2020 ruined the end of his high school career. We chatted over the livestream, as clunky as both learning and teaching were at that time, about what ideas resonated with him and how many of these postmodern ideas rattled him. His question threw me off guard, but I answered as truthfully as I could.

"Well, we're in it now. So that's up to *you,* young man."

He sat silent for a few moments on the video feed.

"All I know is that I know *nothing,*" he finally said with a smile.

I smirked. "He just quoted Socates," I thought. "A student actually listened."

And what's more, he showed me the humility (and humor) that is always ready to assume the posture of a beginner-in-training.

With humility, we can rebuild from this postmodern predicament, brick by brick. We stand upon the shoulders of giants, and we also have been charged to find the good in the day. We cannot retreat into the past. We must move forward with creativity, grounded on the security of a Father who loves His creation and will bless the work we undertake.

The call to have "intellectual charity" is how St. John Paul II challenged us to think: not to wield a weapon of power over reality (à la Bacon and Hobbes) or to gleefully dismantle all notions of order (Foucault and Derrida), but to participate in a playful dance that is curious and receptive, humble and yet firm on the foundation of the Truth.

Wonder is the antidote. We are stewards of what is bestowed on us, not its lords. Therefore, we must care for the time given to us. We can embrace the subjective stories of others and share our own as well. Having the privilege of serving as a teacher, I'm often reminded that the old saying is true: students don't care how much we know until they know how much we care. Listen to one another and share your own heart. Be firm in the foundation we have been given and in the fact that truth can be known and beauty will triumph over chaos.

Exactly how we go at this task will be unique to every individual. We need to try and see the possibility of the good in every situation and certainly the goodness in the human person before us. We can call out poor ideas while still affirming the inherent goodness of every man or woman we're encountering. Every family must discern what steps are best to preserve, protect, and form their household. There are indeed times to circle the wagons and retreat from the madness of the world, times when families relocate, leave the indoctrination of state schools, or pull back from certain modes of entertainment that offer more poison than mirth. There is also the call to be a light in the darkness and a city on a hill, offering a beacon of clarity to the confused (Matt. 5:14).

Jesus did not call us to be isolationists. We are part of His rescue mission. In *Fides et Ratio,* St. John Paul II called on philosophers to recover wisdom and truth so as to formulate the genuine ethics and ideas needed for this time. He also called ordinary men and women to look deeply into the mystery of existence and seek the love of Christ:

> The human being … can find fulfillment only in choosing to enter the truth, to make a home under the shade of Wisdom and dwell there. Only within this horizon of truth will people understand their freedom in its fullness and their call to know and love God as the supreme realization of their true self. . . .
>
> May Mary, Seat of Wisdom, be a sure haven for all who devote their lives to the search for wisdom. May their journey into wisdom, sure and final goal of all true knowing, be freed of every hindrance by the intercession of the one who, in giving birth to the Truth and treasuring it in her heart, has shared it forever with all the world.[89]

[89] John Paul II, *Fides et Ratio*, nos. 107–108.

Appendix

Recommended Reading

FOR ANYONE WHO desires to dive deeper into philosophy, here are some recommended readings. There's no substitute for going straight to the source texts—say, actually trying to read Plato's *Republic* or Augustine's *City of God*—but it helps to have guides who can adequately communicate and simplify these works for our (post)modern minds.

I include a few choice texts from Peter Kreeft, but honestly, reading *any* of his books will bless you in your search for truth.

General Philosophy

- ✠ Norman Melchert. *The Great Conversation*, volumes 1 and 2. Oxford University Press.
- ✠ Richard Tarnas. *The Passion of the Western Mind: Understanding the Ideas That Have Shaped Our World View*. Ballantine Books.
- ✠ Julián Marías. *History of Philosophy.* Dover Books.
- ✠ Jacques Maritain. *An Introduction to Philosophy.* Sheen & Ward.
- ✠ Peter Kreeft. *Socrates' Children: An Introduction to Philosophy from the 100 Greatest Philosophers*, volumes 1–4. Word on Fire.

Postmodernity

- ✠ Carl R. Trueman. *Strange New World: How Thinkers and Activists Redefined Identity and Sparked the Sexual Revolution.* Crossway
- ✠ Stephen R. C. Hicks. *Explaining Postmodernism: Skepticism and Socialism from Rousseau to Foucault.* Ockham's Razor Publishing.
- ✠ Stanley J. Grenz. *A Primer on Postmodernism.* William B. Eerdmans Publishing Company.
- ✠ Abigail Favale. *The Genesis of Gender: A Christian Theory.* Ignatius Press.
- ✠ Helen Pluckrose and James Lindsay. *Cynical Theories: How Activist Scholarship Made Everything about Race, Gender, and Identity—and Why This Harms Everybody.* Pitchstone Publishing.
- ✠ Voddie T. Baucham Jr. *Fault Lines: The Social Justice Movement and Evangelicalism's Looming Catastrophe.* Salem Books
- ✠ Alisa Childers and Tim Barnett. *The Deconstruction of Christianity: What It Is, Why It's Destructive, and How to Respond.* Tyndale House Publishing.
- ✠ C. S. Lewis. *The Abolition of Man.* Harper One.
- ✠ Michael D. O'Brien. *The Family and the New Totalitarianism.* Divine Providence Press.

Resources for Restoration

- ✠ St. Pope John Paul II. *Fides et Ratio* (Faith and Reason). Papal encyclical.
- ✠ Peter Kreeft. *Back to Virtue.* Ignatius Press.
- ✠ Fulton J. Sheen. *Old Errors and New Labels.* St. Paul's Press.
- ✠ Viktor E. Frankl. *Man's Search for Meaning.* Beacon Press.
- ✠ *From Christendom to Apostolic Mission: Pastoral Strategies for an Apostolic Age.* University of Mary Press.
- ✠ Josef Pieper. *Leisure: The Basis of Culture.* Ignatius Press.
- ✠ Christopher West. *At the Heart of the Gospel: Reclaiming the Body for the New Evangelization.* Image Books.
- ✠ Carrie Gress. *The Anti-Mary Exposed: Rescuing the Culture from Toxic Femininity.* TAN Books.
- ✠ Deacon Harold Burke-Sivers. *Building a Civilization of Love: A Catholic Response to Racism.* Ignatius Press.
- ✠ A. G. Sertillanges. *The Intellectual Life: Its Spirit, Conditions, Methods.* Catholic University of America Press.

About the Author

Bobby Angel is an author, speaker, and personal mentor trained by the CatholicPsych Institute. He taught theology and philosophy while serving as a high school minister for almost a decade. Bobby and his wife, Jackie, present regularly on the topics of Christian marriage and discernment and minister through podcasts and media on YouTube. Bobby has authored *Gaming and the Heroic Life* and co-authored *Pray, Decide, and Don't Worry* alongside his wife and Fr. Mike Schmitz. Bobby and Jackie live in Dallas, Texas, with their five children.

Sophia Institute

SOPHIA INSTITUTE IS a nonprofit institution that seeks to nurture the spiritual, moral, and cultural life of souls and to spread the gospel of Christ in conformity with the authentic teachings of the Roman Catholic Church.

Sophia Institute Press fulfills this mission by offering translations, reprints, and new publications that afford readers a rich source of the enduring wisdom of mankind.

Sophia Institute also operates the popular online resource CatholicExchange.com. *Catholic Exchange* provides world news from a Catholic perspective as well as daily devotionals and articles that will help readers to grow in holiness and live a life consistent with the teachings of the Church.

In 2013, Sophia Institute launched Sophia Institute for Teachers to renew and rebuild Catholic culture through service to Catholic education. With the goal of nurturing the spiritual, moral, and cultural life of souls, and an abiding respect for the role and work of teachers, we strive to provide materials and programs that are at once enlightening to the mind and ennobling to the heart; faithful and complete, as well as useful and practical.

Sophia Institute gratefully recognizes the Solidarity Association for preserving and encouraging the growth of our apostolate over the course of many years. Without their generous and timely support, this book would not be in your hands.

www.SophiaInstitute.com
www.CatholicExchange.com
www.SophiaTeachers.org

Sophia Institute Press is a registered trademark of Sophia Institute.
Sophia Institute is a tax-exempt institution as defined by the Internal Revenue Code, Section 501(c)(3). Tax ID 22-2548708.